Alexander Sergunin and Valery Konyshev

RUSSIA IN THE ARCTIC

Hard or Soft Power?

ibidem-Verlag
Stuttgart

Bibliografische Information der Deutschen Nationalbibliothek
Die Deutsche Nationalbibliothek verzeichnet diese Publikation in der Deutschen Nationalbibliografie; detaillierte bibliografische Daten sind im Internet über http://dnb.d-nb.de abrufbar.

Bibliographic information published by the Deutsche Nationalbibliothek
Die Deutsche Nationalbibliothek lists this publication in the Deutsche Nationalbibliografie; detailed bibliographic data are available in the Internet at http://dnb.d-nb.de.

Cover picture: © Pink floyd88 a. Source: https://commons.wikimedia.org/wiki/File:Yamal_2009.JPG. Licensed under CC-BY-SA 3.0 (s. http://creativecommons.org/licenses/by-sa/3.0/deed.en).

∞

Gedruckt auf alterungsbeständigem, säurefreien Papier
Printed on acid-free paper

ISSN: 1614-3515

ISBN-13: 978-3-8382-0753-7

© *ibidem*-Verlag
Stuttgart 2016

Alle Rechte vorbehalten

Das Werk einschließlich aller seiner Teile ist urheberrechtlich geschützt. Jede Verwertung außerhalb der engen Grenzen des Urheberrechtsgesetzes ist ohne Zustimmung des Verlages unzulässig und strafbar. Dies gilt insbesondere für Vervielfältigungen, Übersetzungen, Mikroverfilmungen und elektronische Speicherformen sowie die Einspeicherung und Verarbeitung in elektronischen Systemen.

All rights reserved. No part of this publication may be reproduced, stored in or introduced into a retrieval system, or transmitted, in any form, or by any means (electronic, mechanical, photocopying, recording or otherwise) without the prior written permission of the publisher. Any person who does any unauthorized act in relation to this publication may be liable to criminal prosecution and civil claims for damages.

Printed in Germany

Table of contents

Acknowledgements 7

Acronyms 11

Introduction 15

Chapter 1.
Russian National Interests in the Arctic. 27

Chapter 2.
Russia's Discourse on the High North. 35

Chapter 3.
Russia's Arctic Doctrines. 41

Chapter 4.
The Russian Arctic:
in Search of a Sustainable Development Strategy...................49

    The problem of definition..49
    Climate change's implications for the AZRF......................52
    Conclusion 57

Chapter 5.
Paradiplomacy: a Joker? 59

    Local goes global..59
    Paradiplomacy: strategies and methods 62
    The Institutional framework 72
    Implications of paradiplomacy..77
    Conclusion 78

Chapter 6.
Northern Sea Route. 81

Chapter 7.
Russia's Relations with Major Arctic Players. 89

    U.S.-Russia 90
    Canada-Russia 94
    Russia-Norway 103
    Russia-Denmark 106
    Russia's relations with East Asian countries 107
    NATO and Russia in the Arctic 109
    EU, Russia and the Arctic 113

Chapter 8.
Russia and the Territorial Disputes in the High North 117

    The U.S.-Russian dispute on the Bering Sea 117
    The Russian-Norwegian dispute on the Barents Sea. 127
    Problems Pertaining to Svalbard 136
    Russian Claims on the Arctic Continental Shelf 139

Chapter 9.
Russian Military Strategies in the Arctic. 143

    Threat perceptions 143
    Military activities and modernization plans 146

Conclusions 155

References 159

Acknowledgements

This book resulted from various research and educational projects. In 1993, 1996–98 and 2000–2003 several projects on Russian policies in Northern Europe were implemented with the generous grant support of the Copenhagen Peace Research Institute (COPRI).[1] We remain indebted to the late Professor Håkan Wiberg, ex-Director of COPRI, who played a key role in launching and executing the above-mentioned projects by being its principal consultant and by providing us with useful advice at all their stages. We also extend special thanks to Pertti Joenniemi, Senior Research Fellow, COPRI/DIIS and Karelian Institute, University of Eastern Finland, for his extensive and insightful comments and suggestions during our work on the projects.

In cooperation with the Russian Institute for Strategic Studies (RISS) and Russian International Affairs Council (RIAC) a series of research projects on Russia's relations with the Arctic and non-Arctic actors has been implemented in 2010–2014. These projects have been particularly helpful in understanding Russia's national interests in the High North as well as specificities of Moscow's bilateral relations with various regional players. A deeper insight in Russia's Arctic policy making has also resulted from these research activities. One of the projects with RIAC was of an educational character and resulted in producing a three-volume anthology/reader on Arctic politics[2] as well as course syllabus and teaching manual based on this publication.

In 2012–2013, the project titled "The Arctic: avoiding a new Cold War" and funded by the International Discussion Club "Valdai" has been implemented by an international team under the leadership of Prof. Lassi Heininen, University of Lapland. Some ideas that have been generated and discussed in the context of

---

1 Merged with the Danish Institute for International Studies (DIIS) in 2003.
2 Ivanov, Igor (ed.). 2013. *Arkticheskiy Region: Problemy Mezhdunarodnogo Sotrudnichestva* [The Arctic Region: the Problems of International Cooperation]. Moscow: Aspect Press.

this project are now reflected in this book. Particularly, we are grateful to the project team for testing the theoretical approaches applicable to the Arctic politics and Russian foreign policy behavior.

Since 2013 a project titled "Arctic Urban Sustainability in Russia" run jointly by the Barents Institute at the University of Tromsø (Aileen A Espíritu) and George Washington University (Marlene Laruelle and Robert Orttung) is being implemented with our participation. It was especially helpful in understanding the role of the Russian subnational units in the country's Arctic policy making.

Our participation in the *Global Arctic* project launched in 2014 and run by the Thematic Network on Geopolitics and Security (Prof. Lassi Heininen) has provided us with a global vision of the Arctic and new approach to human security in the region.

It is a pleasant duty to mention here our gratitude to many colleagues who have helped us with especially useful advice or materials for this book. They include: Prof. Rasmus Gjedssø Bertelsen, Barents Chair in Politics, and Piotr Graczyk, University of Tromsø-The Arctic University of Norway; Dr. Rob Huebert, University of Calgary, Canada; Prof. Tapani Kaakkuriniemi and Dr. Hanna Smith, Aleksanteri Institute, University of Helsinki; Prof. Alexander Kubyshkin, St. Petersburg State University; Prof. Roar Kvam, Trondheim Business School, Norway; Gunnar Lassinantti, ex-Project Leader, Olof Palme International Center (Stockholm); Professor Marina Lebedeva, Chair, Department of World Politics, and Prof. Lev Voronkov, Moscow State Institute of International Relations (MGIMO); Prof. Kari Liuhto, Turku School of Economics, University of Turku, Finland; Dr. Natalia Loukacheva, University of North British Columbia, Canada; Arild Moe, Acting Director, Fridtjof Nansen Institute, Norway; Dr. Ingmar Oldberg, Senior Research Fellow, FOA (National Defense Establishment) and Swedish Institute of International Affairs; Mikhail Rykhtik, Director, Institute of International Relations and World History (IIRWH), Nizhny Novgorod State University (NNSU); Professor Poul Wolffsen, Roskilde University (Denmark); Jian Yang, Vice-President, Baozhi Cheng and Pei Zhang, Research Fellows, Shanghai Institutes for

International Studies, China; Dr. Gleb Yarovoy, Petrozavodsk State University, and Dr. Andrei Zagorsky, Institute of World Economy and International Relations, Russian Academy of Science.

We are thankful to a number of research centers and institutions—the School of International Relations, St. Petersburg State University; Department of Political Science, Higher School of Economics, St. Petersburg campus; IIRWH NNSU; the Department of International Relations & Political Science, Nizhny Novgorod Linguistic University, Russia; COPRI/DIIS, Denmark; Stockholm International Peace Research Institute, Sweden; Aleksanteri Institute and Department of Politics, University of Helsinki, which provided us with excellent research environments and warm hospitality. Without their liberal support and help this work was not possible.

Alexander Sergunin
Valery Konyshev
St. Petersburg State University, Russia
July 2015

Acronyms

ABM	Anti-ballistic missile
AC	Arctic Council
AEPS	Arctic Environment Protection Strategy
AGF	Arctic Group of Forces
AMAP	Arctic Monitoring and Assessment Program
AZRF	Arctic Zone of the Russian Federation
BEAC	Barents Euro-Arctic Council
BEAR	Barents Euro-Arctic Region
BRC	Barents Regional Council
BRICS	Brazil, Russia, India, China, South Africa
CBC	Cross-border cooperation
CFSP	Common Foreign and Security Policy
COPRI	Copenhagen Peace Research Institute
CRBC	Canada-Russia Business Council
CTA	City Twins Association
CSBM	Confidence and security building measure
DIIS	Danish Institute for International Studies
EEZ	Exclusive economic zone
ENPI	European Neighborhood Partnership Instrument
ETC	European Territorial Cooperation
EU	European Union
FOA	National Defense Establishment
FSS	Federal Security Service
ICBM	Intercontinental ballistic missile

ICJ	International Court of Justice
IEC	Intergovernmental Economic Commission
IIRWH	Institute of International Relations and World History
IMO	International Maritime Organization
INTERREG	EU's program on interregional co-operation
IR	International Relations
IRSP	Ice-resistant stationary platform
MGIMO	Moscow State Institute of International Relations
NATO	North Atlantic Treaty Organisation
NWSP	North-Western Strategic Partnership
NCM	Nordic Council of Ministers
ND	Northern Dimension
NEFCO	Nordic Environment Finance Corporation
NGO	Non-governmental organization
NNSU	Nizhny Novgorod State University
NORAD	North American Aerospace Defense Command
NSR	Northern Sea Route
PGE	Platinum-group element
POS	Permanent observer status
PTT	Power transition theory
RADARSAT	Canadian space satellite
RAIPON	Russian Association of Indigenous Peoples of the North, Siberia and the Far East
RIAC	Russian International Affairs Council

RISS	Russian Institute for Strategic Studies
SAR	Search and rescue operation
SDS	Sustainable development strategy
SEZ	Special economic zone
SME	Small and medium size enterprises
SWOT	Strengths, weaknesses, opportunities and threads
TBC	Transborder cooperation
Tu	Tupolev
UK	United Kingdom
UN	United Nations
UNCLCS	United Nations Commission on the Limits of the Continental Shelf
UNCLOS	United Nations Convention on the Law of the Seas
UNESCO	United Nations Educational, Scientific and Cultural Organization
UNIDO	United Nations Industrial Development Organization
US	United States
USD	US dollar
USSR	Union of the Soviet Socialist Republics

Introduction

Contending views on Russia's Arctic strategy. The Kremlin's strategy in the High North is a vexed question both in the media and research literature. Russia's decision to plant a titanium flag at the bottom of the Arctic Ocean on the North Pole in August 2007 and resume strategic bomber and navy patrols in the High North, as well as the publication of its first Arctic strategy in 2008, has led some Western experts to criticize Russia's Arctic policies as expansionist, aggressive, and an example of "gunboat diplomacy" (Kraska 2009, 1117; Schepp and Traufetter 2009; Willett 2009, 53). According to some Western analysts, due to Russia's economic weakness and technological backwardness, it tends to emphasize coercive military instruments to protect its national interests in the Arctic, which will inevitably lead to a regional arms race, remilitarization and military conflicts in the High North (Borgerson 2008; Huebert 2010; Huebert et al. 2012; Macalister 2010; Smith and Giles 2007).

However, in contrast with the Cold War era, when Soviet behavior was driven by ideological or geopolitical factors, current Russian policies in the Arctic are explained by Moscow's pragmatic interests such as competition for natural resources and/or control of northern sea routes.

On the other hand, there are authors (mostly Russian but also some Western ones) who see Russia's intentions in the Arctic as innocent, inward-looking, purely defensive, and oriented toward the protection of its legitimate interests (Alexandrov 2009; Belov 2012; Diev 2009; Grigoriev 2010; Khramchikhin 2011 and 2013; Nenashev 2010; Oreshenkov 2009); or who at least see Russia's national intentions in the context of international Arctic cooperation as comparable to other Arctic states (e.g. Heininen 2011). This group of experts emphasizes the fact that Moscow's primary interest is the development of the Arctic Zone of the Russian Federation (AZRF), which is rich in natural resources and underdeveloped in terms of the local economy, infrastructure, communication systems, social institutions and culture. They contend that Moscow is not pursuing a revisionist policy in the Arctic; on the contrary, Russia wants to solve all disputes in the region by peaceful means, relying on international law and international organizations.

There is also a noisy but marginal group of anti-Western writers in Russia who are not afraid to champion Russia as a revisionist, expansionist or imperial state—and not only in the Arctic (Dugin 1991, 1993 and 2002; Indzhiev 2010). They believe that Moscow's Arctic policy must be assertive and proactive to resist the Western 'encroachment' on 'Russia's Arctic' and a multitude of anti-Russian conspiracies. They even criticize the Russian government for lacking a sound and assertive strategy in the region, or for making concessions to other international players (for example, the 2010 Russian-Norwegian treaty on delimitation of maritime territories, or granting a number of non-Arctic states with permanent observer status in the Arctic Council).

The vast majority of authors are either too anti-Russian or openly pro-Russian in their analysis of Russia's strategy and policies in the post-Cold War Arctic. But there are quite a few works that try to objectively analyze Russian interests, motivation, behavior and strategies in the Arctic (Gorenburg 2011; Heininen 2011; Konyshev and Sergunin 2011a, 2012 and 2014; Laruelle 2014; Lasserre, Le Roy and Garon 2012; Voronkov 2012; Zagorsky 2011; Yarovoy 2014). This study continues this tradition and aims to provide a comprehensive picture and analysis of the current situation in the Arctic, as well as a rigorous assessment of the interests and problems of the Russian Federation in the Arctic, particularly the Russian Arctic.

Theoretical framework. The dichotomy of revisionist *vs.* status quo states stems from the realist/neo-realist *power transition theory* (PTT) by A.F.K. Organski (1958) and his followers (Wittkopf 1997; Tammen 2000). This theory aimed at explaining the causes of international conflicts and wars by the rise of emerging powers that were discontent with international rules established by the dominant powers. According to this theory, powerful and influential nations such as the U.S. who have benefited from the previously established world order fall under the category of status quo states while nations dissatisfied with their place on the international spectrum are often considered revisionist states. The PTT was based on the assumption that the revisionist state aims at either a radical change of old rules or imposing new rules on other international actors.

While this theory that was mainly designed for the Cold War period can still probably work in some cases even in the present-day world, it is hardly applicable to the regions such as the Arctic. None of the regional players can be considered as purely status quo or revisionist power. The five coastal states (Canada, Denmark, Norway, Russia and the U.S.) hardly can be considered as status quo/dominant powers who want to impose its own regional order on other players and whose positions are challenged by the rising powers. Their legitimate rights to have exclusive economic zones (EEZs) in the Arctic Ocean are not questioned by other states. At the same time, from the PPT perspective, the Arctic-5 themselves can be seen as revisionist powers because Canada, Denmark, Russia and the U.S. have ambitions to extend their EEZs (Norway has already done this in 2009), i.e. to change existing rules. But in contrast with the PTT postulates, these quasi-revisionist states aim at solving disputable questions in a 'civilized' way, through international institutions, particularly, in the framework of the UN Commission on the Limits of Continental Shelf (UNCLCS). Moreover, as the Ilulissat Declaration of 2008 proclaimed, the Arctic-5 intend to solve all disputes by peaceful methods through negotiations and on the basis of international law.

Other regional players also demonstrate a mixture of revisionist and status quo behavior. For example, on the one hand, three sub-Arctic (Finland, Iceland and Sweden) and non-Arctic states (especially the East Asian ones) are unhappy with the rules that the Arctic-5 tend to establish in the region. They try to elevate their statuses by becoming either full-fledged members of the regional organizations (the former three countries) or permanent observers (the latter ones). On the other hand, in some areas these actors tend to be status quo powers. For instance, they prefer to keep the current situation with the EEZs in the High North unchangeable because some 'lucrative pieces' of the Arctic continental shelf (e.g. the Lomonosov and Mendeleev underwater ridges which are allegedly rich in oil and gas) are located in *terra et aqua nullius* (nobody's lands and waters) and theoretically—if their legal status remains legally indefinite—they can be exploited by everyone who has money and technologies for doing this.

It should be noted that, in fact, a real multipolar system exists now in the Arctic, the regional order that cannot be explained with the help of the PTT because it was designed for the Cold War-type hierarchical (bipolar) system.

One more problem with the revisionist/status quo powers theory is that it ignores the existence of the third type of states—the reformist one. Similar to the revisionist powers this kind of states is unsatisfied with the existing rules of the 'game' but they do not want to change them radically; rather they aim at reforming them to adapt them to the new realities and make them more comfortable for all the members of world or regional community. Such states prefer to act on the basis of existing rules and norms rather than challenge them. All changes (reforms) should be made gradually, through negotiations and to the benefit of all the parties involved. It is safe to assume that all the Arctic states (and even the non-Arctic countries) perfectly fall into this category, including Russia. One can distinguish between more or less assertive reformist actors but even most assertive ones hardly can be seen as revisionist states.

The concept of a reformist state is relatively new in the International Relations (IR) literature. Scholars prefer to call them 'pluralist', 'non-aligned', etc. The concept of 'coexistence' (but without its Marxist connotation) has recently become again popular in the IR literature with regard to the emerging powers (such as the BRICS countries) (De Coning 2014; Odgaard 2012). According to this school, countries with completely different socio-economic and political systems can peacefully coexist. The emerging powers agree to play by existing rules but want to make them more just and adequate to the changing realities (Nadkarni and Noonan 2013). They do not accept a dominant state (states) imposing rules on the rest of the world and favor a multipolar world model. The 'coexistence' concept quite nicely fits the reformist state's political philosophy and can be applicable to the explanation of foreign policy behavior of many newly emerging powers, including Russia.

It should be noted that the type of actor does not tell much about the style of its behavior or instruments used to achieve its goals. The status quo state may be violent in protecting its interests and international positions while the revisionist state—for various reasons—may prefer non-coercive instruments such as diplomacy or economic leverages.

To explain the changing meaning of power in the present-day world and new patterns of behavior of the key international actors, new theories have emerged in the post-Cold War era. The soft power concept coined by Joseph Nye is one of the new generation theories that to our understanding can be helpful in understanding Russia's Arctic strategies.

According to this school, in the post-Cold War period key international players prefer to exercise 'soft' rather than 'hard' power because the economic, socio-cultural, institutional and legal instruments are much more efficient now than the military strength or direct political pressure. For Nye, the author of the concept, the soft power is, first and foremost, an ability to be attractive. The soft power of a country rests primarily on three resources: "its culture (in places where it is attractive to others), its political values (when it lives up to them at home and abroad), and its foreign policies (when they are seen as legitimate and having moral authority)" (Nye 2004: 11).

The Russian theorists and policy-makers suggested their own versions of the soft power theory. For example, with regard to the Russian sector of the Arctic they make emphasis on economic attractiveness of the region because of its vast natural resources and shorter sea and air routes. For President Vladimir Putin, soft power is a sort of a PR technology that helps either to lobby Moscow's interests in foreign countries or improve Russia's international image (Putin 2012a and Putin 2012b). The most recent Russian Foreign Policy Concept (12 February 2013) defines the 'soft' power as a "complex set of instruments to achieve foreign policy aims by means of the civil society, information, communicative, humanitarian and other methods and technologies that are different from classical diplomacy" (Putin 2013a). It is important to note that irrespectively how the Kremlin interprets the soft power concept and whether it is in tune with Nye's original definition Moscow has no intention to use coercive instruments in its Arctic policies and be a trouble-maker in the region.

To sum up the theoretical part of our study we'd like to emphasize that this research is based on two assumptions/hypotheses: First, Russia is a reformist rather than status quo or revisionist state in the Arctic. Second, Russia tries to be a soft rather than hard power in the High North. The research below aims at examining these key hypotheses.

Research agenda. This study seeks to determine whether Russia is really a revisionist power in the Arctic, or whether it is interested in regional stability and international cooperation in the High North. To answer this question, a number of smaller questions must be discussed:

- What are Russia's real interests in the Arctic, as opposed to its rhetoric regarding the region?
- How do different schools of thought on Russian foreign policy understand the problems posed by the Arctic?
- What is the conceptual/doctrinal basis for Russia's Arctic strategy?
- How does Russia build relations with major Arctic and non-Arctic actors in the region?
- What is Moscow's political approach to working within international organizations and fora that deal with Arctic issues?

- How does Russia address major Arctic challenges such as climate change, environmental degradation, territorial claims and division of the continental shelf, the use of sea routes, etc.?
- What are Russia's real military policies and plans in the Arctic? Do they pose a security threat to other Arctic players, or are Moscow's limited military preparations and activities in keeping with the existing regional military balance?

Sources. This paper is based on the following sources:

- International documents (treaties, agreements, resolutions, etc.).
- Governmental/official publications and materials (Russian and Western).
- Published interviews with officials, politicians, NGO leaders, and experts.
- Statistical information, yearbooks, guides, and reference books.
- Research literature: monographs, analytical papers, and articles.
- Media publications.

As with any study of 'hot' political issues, it's difficult to find reliable data. Information is often classified, misleading, or not fully reported. A scholar has to corroborate data from numerous unconfirmed media reports.

Research is further complicated by differences of opinion among experts on methods of statistical analysis. Moreover, research techniques and terminology can vary. Therefore, we have relied on our critical judgment and a careful comparison of sources in compiling the database for this research. Since it involves not only data collection but also data analysis, we relied on three main criteria for selecting and interpreting sources:

- Validity: Data must represent the most important and characteristic trends rather than occasional or irregular developments.

- Informativeness: Sources that provide valuable and timely information are given priority.
- Innovativeness: Preference is given to sources that offer original data, fresh ideas, and untraditional approaches.

These research techniques are helpful in overcoming the limitations of available sources and compiling substantial and sufficient data for the study.

Structure of the book. The book consists of an introduction, nine chapters, conclusions and bibliography.

The *first chapter* demonstrates that Russia has important economic, societal, environmental and military-strategic interests in the High North. These interests include the access, exploration and development of the Arctic natural resources (especially the hydrocarbon ones). Russia tries to modernize and further develop the AZRF's industrial base which makes a significant and valuable contribution to the country's economy. Moscow is also interested in opening up of the Northern Sea Route (NSR) for international commercial traffic and developing circumpolar air routes. Moscow is deeply concerned about the debilitating ecological system in the AZRF and trying to stop and reverse the negative trends in this sphere. Russia still has considerable military-strategic interests in the region. These have not lost their relevance with the end of the Cold War. This continuity can clearly be seen in Russia's security perceptions of the Arctic as a region of both challenges and opportunities.

Chapter 2 examines the Russian post-Soviet debate on the Arctic. It is argued that despite the continuing prevalence of the realist and geopolitical schools the Russian discourse on the High North became much more diverse, creative and interesting than fifteen-twenty years ago. A number of alternative schools have emerged, namely—neo-liberalism, globalism, critical geopolitics and social constructivism. Nowadays, the Russian decision-makers, facing a rather diverse intellectual landscape, can get expertise on the Arctic issues from different schools and groupings.

Chapter 3 analyzes the evolution of the Russian Arctic doctrinal/conceptual frameworks in the post-Soviet period. The Russian

Arctic strategies of 2008 and 2013 are characterized. The conceptual/doctrinal basis of Russia's Arctic strategy has turned out to be less ambitious and aggressive, and more realistic and cooperative in spirit, than many might have expected. Russia's most recent Arctic strategy (February 2013) is more inward-looking than expansionist. Regarding the international dimension, Moscow's Arctic policy calls for international cooperation, multilateral diplomacy.

At the same time, the chapter argues that the Strategy-2013 is a good invitation to further discussions on Russia's Arctic policies rather than a comprehensive and sound doctrine. To become an efficient national strategy in the region it should be further clarified, specified and instrumentalized in a series of federal laws, regulations and task programs. It should be also better designed for the international consumption.

Chapter 4 focuses on the Russian sustainable development strategy in the Arctic. The authors note that the Russian academic community has managed to develop a comprehensive vision of the Arctic sustainable development which is based on the combination of different interpretations of sustainable development— economic, ecological and social/human. Such an integrated approach has been reflected in the Russian doctrinal documents, including the most recent ones. Numerous efforts have been made over the last two decades to solve most acute environmental problems of the AZRF, including the programs on stopping or limiting pollution in Russia's major industrial centers and environmental clean-up on the Arctic islands.

It is argued, however, that the course toward a combination of modernization and innovation with sustainable development charted by the Russian government should move from making declarations to the implementation phase involving specific, realistic and the same time environmentally friendly projects in the AZRF.

In the *fifth chapter,* the phenomenon of paradiplomacy of the Russian Arctic subnational actors is explored. Particularly, this chapter examines how paradiplomacy is exploited by the Russian Arctic subnational actors (regions and municipalities) for building their sustainable development strategy. More specifically, three research questions are addressed: First, what are the actors' incentives for subnational international activities? Second, what are the main paradiplomatic strategies, instruments and institutions? Third, what are the negative and positive implications of paradiplomacy for the center-periphery relations and Russia's foreign policy? The chapter focuses on the following strategies/methods of paradiplomacy: making direct agreements with international partners; attracting foreign investment; creating a positive image of the regions; cooperation with international organizations; establishing representative offices in foreign countries; city-twinning; participation in subregional arrangements; capitalizing on national diplomacy and federal infrastructures, etc. The authors conclude that in the foreseeable future paradiplomacy will retain its importance for the subnational actors of the Russian Arctic as an efficient instrument for building sustainable development strategies.

Chapter 6 is devoted to the analysis of competitive advantages and disadvantaged of the NSR. Despite some serious obstacles to the NSR's exploitation as an international sea lane, it will remain a priority for Russia's strategy in the Arctic region in the foreseeable future. The Kremlin considers the NSR an effective resource for developing the AZRF both domestically and internationally. For this reason, Moscow plans to make considerable investments in the NSR and bring its infrastructure in line with international standards. However, as with other aspects of its Arctic policy, Russia faces a difficult dilemma: how to maintain control over the NSR while also opening it up to international cooperation and integration with the global transportation system.

Chapter 7 addresses Russia's policies towards key Arctic powers (U.S., Canada, Norway and Denmark), emerging Arctic powers from East Asia (China, Japan and South Korea), and international organizations which are eager to become active circumpolar actors (NATO and the EU). It is argued that Moscow pursues a differentiated policy towards these players. While the Kremlin tries to build partnership-type relations with other Arctic coastal states, it is rather cautious with regard to the newcomers from East Asia, overtly negative to NATO and lukewarm to the EU. It is argued that even in those cases when Moscow is displeased with the Arctic actors' behavior or intentions it tries to avoid an open confrontation with them and prefers dialogue with all regional players.

In the *eight chapter,* territorial disputes in the High North (with Russia's participation) are examined. These conflicts are seen by the Russian strategists as a significant threat to the country's security. The Arctic region has inherited a number of territorial disputes from the Cold War era and Russia was a party to them. Some of these conflicts were successfully settled down while others are still waiting for their resolution. This chapter addresses four cases: the U.S.-Soviet/Russian dispute on the Bering Sea; the Norwegian-Russian dispute on the Barents Sea delimitation which was successfully resolved in 2010; the Svalbard question which is another Norwegian-Russian disputable issue, and the Russian claim on the extension of its continental shelf in the Arctic Ocean. The chapter concludes that despite these disputes Moscow believes that the territorial problems should be solved through negotiations and on the basis of international law.

Chapter 9 aims at analysis of the Russian military strategies in the High North. In contrast with a widespread perception of Russia as an expansionist power in the Arctic, the authors argue that Moscow does not seek military superiority in the region. They note that the Russian military modernization programs are rather modest and aim to upgrading the Russian armed forces in the High North rather than providing them with additional offensive capabilities or restoring the Soviet-time huge military potential. Given the financial constraints these programs have recently become less ambitious and more realistic. They do not violate the regional military balance and do not provoke a new round of of arms race in the Arctic. The Russian military increasingly aims at defending the country's economic interests in the region and control over the huge AZRF territory rather than expanding its 'sphere of influence'.

Chapter 1.
Russian National Interests in the Arctic.

Russia has numerous, multidimensional national interests in the Arctic region, and the entire North. Russia's interests in the Arctic can be grouped into the following categories:

Access to natural resources. First and foremost, the Arctic is attractive to Russia for its vast natural resources. According to the U.S. Geological Survey (2008), the mean estimate of total undiscovered conventional oil and gas resources in the Arctic is approximately 90 billion barrels of oil, 1.669 trillion cubic feet of natural gas, and 44 billion barrels of natural gas liquids. Arctic deposits total approximately 240 billion barrels of oil and oil-equivalent natural gas, which is almost 10% of the world's known conventional petroleum resources (cumulative production and remaining proved reserves). And yet most of the Arctic, especially offshore, remains essentially unexplored with respect to petroleum.

The AZRF holds most of the Arctic's hydrocarbon reserves (see table 1). This region of Russia is the most prolific producer of Russian gas (95%) and oil (about 70%) (Dobretsov and Pokhilenko 2010). Russian geologists have discovered about 200 oil and gas deposits in the AZRF. There are 22 large shelf deposits in the Barents and Kara seas, which are expected to be developed in the near future (Prirodnye Resursy Arktiki 2010).

The AZRF is also abundant in mineral resources. Its mining industries produce primary and placer diamond (99% of total Russian production), platinum-group elements (PGE) (98%), nickel and cobalt (over 80%), chromium and manganese (90%), copper (60%), antimony, tin, tungsten, and rare metals (from 50 to 90%), and gold (about 40%) (Dobretsov and Pokhilenko 2010). The development of Arctic and subarctic mineral resources is indispensable both for Russia and the world. But this process is very difficult and requires a solid geological, ecological, and economic foundation as well as special approaches (Kontorovich et al., 2010).

Table 1. Distribution of the undiscovered hydrocarbon resources among the Arctic coastal states, %

Country	Oil	Natural gas
Russia	41	70
U.S. (Alaska)	28	14
Greenland (Denmark)	18	8
Canada	9	4
Norway	4	4

Source: Naumov and Nikulkina 2012.

In addition to mineral reserves, the Arctic possesses abundant bio-resources. More than 150 fish species can be found in Arctic waters, including important varieties for Russian (and international) commercial fishing, such as herring, cod, butterfish, haddock and flatfish.

The AZRF produces 15% of Russia's seafood (Kochemasov et al. 2009). The region is also populated by some unique animal species such as the polar bear, narwhal, walrus and white whale.

Industrial significance of the AZRF. A major industrial base was created in the AZRF under the Soviet regime, and includes mining, oil and gas, pipeline systems, electric power stations, the Bilibin nuclear power plant, and extensive transport infrastructure (rail and motor roads, airfields, river and sea ports, etc.). The AZRF is home to 46 towns with populations over 5,000, as well as four cities with populations over 100,000—a record among Arctic coastal states. With just 1% of the country's population, it already accounts for 11% of Russian gross domestic product and 22% of its export revenue (Kochemasov et al. 2009; Schepp and Traufetter 2009). The Russian government and private business intend to restore and further develop the industries and infrastructure of the AZRF, with plans for hundreds of billions in Russian and foreign direct investment in important sectors of the regional economy, such as energy, mining, transport infrastructure and communications (Medvedev 2008; Putin 2013).

A potentially important transport junction. Moreover, if Arctic ice continues to melt, Russia stands to enjoy considerable economic gains from the development and exploitation of the NSR—the shortest shipping route between European and East Asian ports, as well as an important domestic route connecting Siberian river ports as well as the European and Far Eastern parts of the country. Circumpolar air routes between North America and Asia (with transit via Siberian airports) is another promising transport project. Circumpolar air traffic is already growing four times faster than the global average (Kross-Polyarny Express 2008).

Environmental concerns. Moscow is deeply concerned about the environmental situation in the AZRF. As a result of intensive industrial and military activities in the region, many Arctic areas are heavily polluted and pose serious health hazards. Russian scientists identified 27 so-called impact zones where pollution has led to environmental degradation and increased morbidity among the local population (see figure 1). The main impact zones include the Murmansk Region (10% of total pollutants in the 27 impact zones), Norilsk urban agglomeration (more than 30%), West Siberian oil and gas fields (more than 30%) and the Arkhangelsk Region (around 5%) (Dushkova and Evseev 2011; Ekologicheskoe Sostoyanie Impactnykh Raionov 2012). In sum, about 15% of the AZRF territory is polluted or contaminated (Kochemasov et al. 2009).

Russia, along with other Arctic states, is concerned about nuclear safety in the Arctic Region, especially on Arctic seas. Northern Russia, particularly the Barents Sea area, has the largest concentration of nuclear installations—both military and civilian—in the world. More than 80 nuclear submarines with over 200 nuclear reactors were located there at one time (Ahunov 2000, 73). The operational risks of reactors at nuclear power plants in the AZRF (some are the same RBMK model used at Chernobyl) also present a serious threat to the population and a large area of Russia and Europe. Spent nuclear fuel and radioactive waste in Russia is also a widespread and worrying problem (for more details see Heininen and Segerstahl 2002).

Figure 1. The map of impact zones in the Russian Arctic.

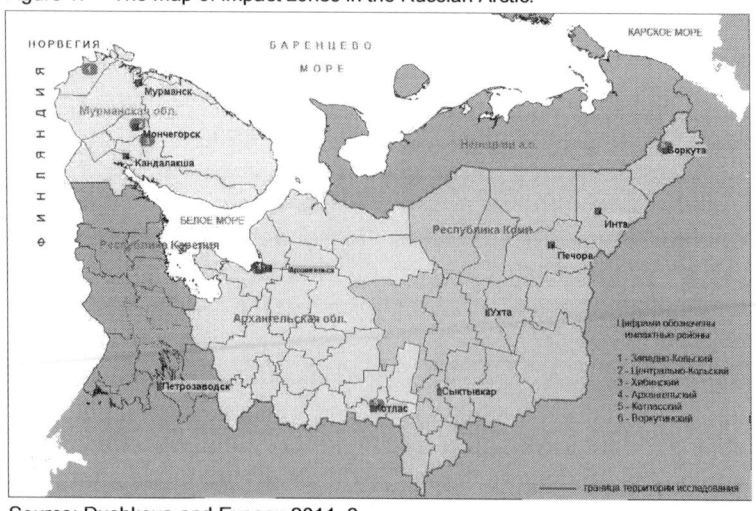

Source: Dushkova and Evseev 2011, 2.

The AZRF is extremely vulnerable to nuclear contamination. Tens of thousands of cubic meters of highly radioactive nuclear waste have collected there. Radioactive material from nuclear munitions factories in Krasnoyarsk, Tomsk, Chelyabinsk used to float down the great Siberian rivers and into the Arctic Ocean. From 1964 to 1991, fluid and solid radioactive waste was dumped in the Barents and Kara seas. According to some reports, the Soviet Union dumped 13 nuclear reactors in the Kara Sea (including 6 with nuclear fuel). Three reactors and a con tainer with nuclear waste from the ice-breaker Lenin were also allegedly dumped in the sea. Radioactive waste amounted to 319,000 curie in the Barents Sea and 2,419,000 curie in the Kara Sea (Ekologicheskoe Sostoyanie Impactnykh Raionov 2012; Gizewski, 1995: 25–41). Although Russia has stopped dumping, the remaining nuclear waste in the Arctic is still a serious problem for the country. With the help of Western partners (especially the Norwegians) Russia is implementing a number of nuclear waste treatment projects in the Murmansk and Arkhangelsk regions.

Indigenous people. Twenty seven indigenous ethnic groups, totaling about 200,000 people, live in the AZRF (Savel'eva and Savel'ev 2010, 75). Improving the quality of life and economic opportunities for indigenous peoples is listed among the strategic priorities of Russia's 2008 Arctic strategy (Medvedev 2008), and further elaborated on in a special document, the Concept for the Sustainable Development of Small Indigenous Population Groups of the North, Siberia and the Far East of the Russian Federation, which was released in February 2009. The document, also called Concept-2009, describes the measures taken by federal and regional authorities in the preceding 15 years, such as federal and regional targeted programs, legislation containing various forms of government support (e.g. incentives, subsidies, and quotas on the use of biological resources), and Russia's active participation in the International Decade of the World's Indigenous People (1995–2004) and the Second International Decade of the World's Indigenous People (2005–2015).

At the same time, Concept-2009 recognizes the serious social and economic problems facing its indigenous peoples (the incompatibility of their traditional way of life with current economic conditions, low competitiveness of traditional economic activities, rising disease rates, a high infant mortality rate, alcoholism, etc.). The unemployment rate among Russia's indigenous people has been estimated at 30–60%, which is 3–4 time higher that among other AZRF residents (Kochemasov et al. 2009). Life expectancy is as low as 49 years, compared to over 60 years on average throughout Russia.

Concept-2009 stated that its implementation should foster favorable conditions for the sustainable development of the indigenous peoples, for example by raising the quality of life to the average in Russia and by halving the infant mortality rate by 2025 compared to 2007 levels.

However, implementation of Concept-2009 has fallen short of these goals, resulting in harsh criticism by Russia's main indigenous organization, the Russian Association of Indigenous Peoples of the North, Siberia and the Far East (RAIPON). RAIPON has called for support from international organizations such as the UN and AC, blaming the Russian government for violating the basic rights of the country's indigenous people. As a result of these efforts, RAIPON's legal registration was suspended by the Russian Ministry of Justice in 2012, and the group had to undergo the rather onerous procedure of re-registering and "cleansing" its leadership of "disloyal elements." This conflict has impeded the further implementation of Concept-2009.

Strategic-military importance. With the end of the Cold War Moscow stopped to perceive the High North as a region of potential military (hard security) confrontation with the NATO/West. The huge Soviet military infrastructure—air, naval and land forces bases, navigation, surveillance and monitor systems, fuel, ammunition and military hardware depots, etc.—has been dismantled or degraded. Air and naval patrols were reduced to the minimum. The number of Russian troops and armaments deployed in the Far North has significantly decreased over the 1990s.

However, with the beginning of international competition for the Arctic natural resources, the launch of (modest) military modernization programs in the neighboring countries, intensification of international organizations' activities in the region (EU and NATO) and non-Arctic states (especially the East Asian ones) and potential rise of new, non-traditional, security threats related to climate change (poaching, smuggling, illegal migration, man-made environmental catastrophes, etc.) Russia's security perception has changed again. On the one hand, there was a return of 'classical'/'old' hard security agenda aimed at responding NATO countries' increased military preparations and activities as well as ascertaining Russia's national sovereignty over 'its' Arctic sector. On the other hand, Moscow is keen on cooperation with other Arctic and non-Arctic states in the field of soft security. It should be also noted that Russia's modernized military infrastructure in the Arctic, including the Soviet air and naval bases which have been reopened over the last years, is of dual-use nature. Such an infrastructure can be used not only for military but also for civilian purposes (for example, for search and rescue (SAR) operations).

The situation has been aggravated by the Ukrainian crisis. Despite the Russian calls on the Western countries to jointly prevent crisis' spill-over effect on the Arctic, the EU and NATO have introduced economic and political sanctions on Russia as well as stopped their cooperation with Moscow in the military sphere. This led to Russia (modest) counter-reaction, including military measures in the High North. The Kremlin has accelerated its military modernization programs and expanded its military activities in the region, including air and sea patrols and military exercises.

Although the whole security situation in the High North has not degenerated to the Cold War-type confrontation, the entire atmosphere in the region is poisoned and the feelings of mistrust and suspicion are again in place. Along with being a platform for international cooperation now the Arctic is again perceived by Moscow as a hypothetic military theatre to be taken care of.

To conclude, Russia has substantial reasons to seek a leading role in the Arctic. It has important economic, social, environmental and military-strategic interests in the region, which Russian officials have vowed to defend.

Chapter 2.
Russia's Discourse on the High North.

Over the last decade the Arctic has become a popular theme for discussions in the Russian academic and expert communities. Along with issues such as the NATO and EU eastward enlargements, a series of 'color revolutions' in the post-Soviet space and Arab world, Russia's current and future roles in the Arctic has become an 'existential question' for the Russian intellectual and political elites. While Moscow in its relations with the West and post-Soviet countries often demonstrates its weakness and inability to set an agenda for a dialogue, the Arctic is seen as a 'dreamland' where Russia can demonstrate its creativity and strength. Moreover, with the help of the Arctic the Russian *intelligentsia* can escape from the perennial identical dilemma: whether Russia is a part of the West or the East? The Arctic suggests an unexpected answer: Russians are neither westerners nor easterners; they are the northerners or *hyperboreans*[3] (Dugin, 1993).

On a more concrete note the Russian discourse on the Arctic may be reduced to the fighting between, on the one hand, normativists and pragmatics and, on the other, alarmists (security-oriented thinkers) and non-alarmists (proponents of the desecuritized approach).

---

3 In ancient Greek mythology the Hyperboreans were mythical people who lived "beyond the North Wind". The Greeks thought that Boreas, the god of the North Wind lived in Thrace, and therefore Hyperborea indicates a region that lay far to the north of Thrace. Later Roman and Byzantine sources continued to change the location of Hyperborea, pointing to Britain, Alps, Central Asia, Urals, Siberia, etc. However, all these sources agreed these were all in the far north of Greece or southern Europe. In the 19–20th centuries, there were numerous pseudo-academic and esoteric schools which claimed the Hyperborean origin of the Indo-European culture or believed that Hyperborea was the Golden Age polar center of civilization and spirituality. In the same vein the present-day Russian romantic-nationalistic school believes that the Russians are modern hyperboreans who differ from the Western people with their materialist/consumerist/individualist culture by spirituality, high moral standards and patriotism.

The first debate is manifested by the clash between the value- and interest-based approaches to the Arctic:

Value-based approach is mostly shared by the Russian version of neo-liberalism. According to this approach, the Arctic (particularly, its natural resources and sea routes) is a common humankind's heritage/asset that should be exploited together with other countries and in a very careful way (Baranovsky, 2002, Leshukov 2001; Zagorsky 2011). The neo-liberals believe that subregional institutions such as the AC and Barents-Euro-Arctic Council (BEAC) are parts of the global and regional governance systems and should be designed and function accordingly. For them, the AC and BEAC should avoid discussion of security issues; rather, environmental issues and the 'human dimension' (indigenous people and other residents of the Arctic regions) should be their main priorities.

Interest-based approach is developed by the Russian neo-realism. According to the neo-realist perspective, Russia's principal interest is to turn the Arctic into its main 'strategic resource base' and other policy considerations should be subordinated to this over-arching goal. Both Russian domestic policies in the AZRF and Moscow's international strategy should be oriented to the protection of its national interests in the region (Alexandrov 2009; Oreshenkov 2010; Voronkov 2012). Against this background it is especially important to secure Russia's economic interests in the Arctic. A variety of various instruments ranging from diplomacy and international arbitration to a modest military build-up and creation of capabilities to effectively prevent poaching and smuggling are suggested. In contrast with the neo-liberals, the neo-realists are quite pragmatic as regards the international institutions such as the UN, AC and BEAC. They do not believe that these international fora are the components of the global or regional governance system whose existence is sharply denied by them. They suggest using these bodies first and foremost to protect Russia's national interests in the region (like other member states do) rather than promote some abstract universal values.

Another division line emerged from the debate on Arctic security. In this sphere two approaches can be distinguished as well:

Securitization approach. This approach is developed by the alarmist-type analysts (mainly from the geopolitical and realist camps) who tend to see every Arctic problem from the national security point of view—be it ecological problems and fisheries or territorial disputes and control over the sea routes. For example, the recent Russian Arctic strategy is partially designed in such an alarmist/securitized way (Putin 2013).

The radical version of this school views the Arctic as a manifestation of the perennial geopolitical rivalry between Russia and the West. In contrast with the past, the West prefers economic rather than military instruments for putting pressure on Russia. The aim of the Western policies is to secure Russia's status of the West's "younger partner" and a source of cheap natural resources and labor force.

Contrary to what has been stated in the Russian official security doctrines, the perception of the U.S. and NATO as the main threats to Russia's security is still alive in large parts of the Russian political, military and expert establishment. Military and diplomatic activities by the U.S. and NATO in the High North are routinely perceived as being of an 'offensive character.'

The extreme (nationalistic) version of this approach sees the Arctic above all as a crucial element in the revival of Russia's great power status and are therefore focused on geopolitical competition with the West, and in particular with the U.S. For example, in his book titled *The Arctic Battle: Will the North be Russian?* Artur Indzhiev has announced the onset of a sort of the Third World War in which a weakened Russia will have to prove its heroism in order to safeguard its rights in the Arctic against aggressive Western powers (Indzhiev 2010). As mentioned above, Alexander Dugin suggests that nowadays the eternal competition between the sea and land powers has been transformed from the geostrategic rivalry to the geoeconomic one (geopolitics of natural resources) (Dugin 1991, 1993 and 2002).

Other authors put forward a more spiritual view of the role of the High North in the construction of Russian identity and the pursuit of its traditional messianism. For instance, in his *The Mysteries of Eurasia*, Dugin (1991) elaborates a cosmogony of the world in order to make Siberia, the last "empire of paradise" after Thule, the instrument of his geopolitical desire for a domination of the world, justified by Russia's "cosmic destiny". This group of theorists claims that the North is not only Russia's strategic resource base (as stated by the Kremlin) but also its territory of the spirit, of heroism, and of overcoming, a symbolic resource of central importance for the future of the country (Laruelle 2014, 39–43).

In both cases, the Arctic is presented as Russia's "last chance," and as a possible way to take "revenge on history." The Arctic is presented as rightful compensation for the hegemony lost with the disappearance of the Soviet Union.

De-securitized (technocratic/instrumentalist) approach. The proponents of this approach believe that most of the Arctic problems can be solved beyond the security context, in a 'normal way'. In case of a conflict, this school suggests to use negotiations to realize positions of the opposite party and find a compromise that could satisfy both contending sides. To this group of analysts, the work on the technical/instrumentalist level has a consolatory effect on the conflicting parties and creates an interdependency mechanism that additionally contributes to the problem-solving process.

The proponents of this approach (mainly from the neo-liberal school) point out that the military significance of the Russian North has dramatically decreased in the post-Cold War period. The region is, in their view, unable to play the role of the Russian military outpost. The neo-liberals hope that the Arctic will be further opened up for international co-operation to become a Russian "gate-way" region that could help Russia to be gradually integrated in the European and world multilateral institutions. They believe that due to its unique geo-economic location the AZRF has a chance to be a "pioneer"/pilot Russian region to be included into the regional and subregional cooperation. They think that a priority should be given to the issues that unite rather than disunite regional players—trade, cross-border co-operation, transport, environment, health care, Arctic research, indigenous people, people-to-people contacts and so on. In this respect, they view the Northern Dimension partnerships as well as AC, BEAC and Nordic institutions' programs as a helpful framework for such co-operation (Baranovsky, 2002, Leshukov 2001; Zagorsky 2011).

The neo-liberals believe that it is very important to guarantee that the Arctic players should interact with each other on the basis of the following principles:

- preserving peace, predictability and stability in the Arctic region,
- ensuring sustainable management and development of natural resources,
- international cooperation to meet common challenges in the Arctic
- developing national and international legal mechanisms to promote Arctic governance.

It should be noted that there are not only differences between various Russian IR schools but also some consensus between them exists. For instance, they tend to agree upon the growing significance of the Arctic both for Russia and the world at large. They also agree that Russia has to have a sound Arctic strategy which should clearly describe Russia's national interests and policy priorities in the region, including both opportunities and limits for international cooperation. The Russian theorists would like to have a flexible Arctic strategy that makes a distinction between Russia's long-, mid- and short-term goals in the region and which is able to quickly adapt to change.

To sum up, the Russian discourse on the Arctic cannot be reduced to the realist and geopolitical paradigms albeit they are still dominant in the Russian foreign policy thinking. This discourse has gradually grown diverse and creative. Now, in terms of expertise, the Russian political leadership faces diversity rather than uniformity and has the option of choosing among different views and options. And the Putin's decision to make emphasis on the soft power instruments in his foreign policy demonstrates that the liberal argumentation has been heard by the Kremlin.

It is important to know that the Russian discourse on the Arctic is rather dynamic and subject to permanent changes. The overtly anti-Western and nationalistic groupings are now marginal and do not really affect the Russian decision-making on the Arctic. At the same time, the role of the open-minded and globally-thinking schools is of growing significance both in the academia and policy-making system. Against this background it is important to provide the Russian discourse on the Arctic with a favorable international environment. When the latter is friendly and cooperative it strengthens the Russian neo-liberal and globalists. And—on the contrary—when bellicose and anti-Russian voices in the West prevail, the Russian geopoliticians and neo-realists become stronger. To prevent the rise of the radical groups in the Russian academic and expert communities a direct dialogue between Russian and foreign specialists should be encouraged through various academic fora and joint research projects.

Chapter 3.
Russia's Arctic Doctrines.

After the collapse of the Soviet Union and prior to the early 2000s the Kremlin paid a little attention to the North. With the end of the Cold War the region has lost its former military-strategic significance for Moscow as a zone of potential confrontation with the NATO/U.S. In the Yeltsin era, the economic potential of the region was underestimated. Moreover, in the 1990s, Russia's northern territories were perceived by the federal government as a burden or source of various socio-economic problems rather than an economically promising region. The far northern regions were almost abandoned by Moscow and had to rely on themselves (or foreign humanitarian assistance) in terms of survival.

The situation started to slowly change in the early 2000s when the general socio-economic situation in Russia has improved and the Putin government with its ambitious agenda of Russia's revival has come to power.

As a result of the increased Kremlin's interest to the High North Russia has become one of the first Arctic states to formulate its strategy in the High North. Only Norway was ahead of Russia in shaping its official Arctic strategy in 2006.

As early as June 14, 2001, the Russian Cabinet had already approved a draft document titled "Foundations of the State Policy of the Russian Federation in the Arctic" (Government of the Russian Federation 2001) which outlineed Russia's national interests and main strategies in the Arctic. But it took another seven years (and another president) to develop a final version of Russia's Arctic strategy.

Strategy-2008. On September 18, 2008, President Medvedev approved the Foundations of the State Policy of the Russian Federation in the Arctic to 2020 and Beyond (Medvedev 2008). The six-page document enumerated Russian national interests in the region: developing the resources of the Arctic; turning the NSR into a unified national transport corridor and line of communication;

and maintaining the region as a zone of international cooperation. According to Russia's plans for the multifaceted development of its northern territories, somewhere between 2016 and 2020 the Arctic was expected to become Russia's "leading strategic resource base."

Russia's strategic security goal for the region was defined as "ensuring a favorable operational regime in the Arctic zone of the Russian Federation, including maintenance of the necessary combat capabilities of general-purpose troops (forces) of the Armed Forces of the Russian Federation and other troops, military formations, and military agencies in this region." This involved strengthening the Coastal Defense Service of the Federal Security Service (FSS) and border controls in the AZRF, and establishing technical control at straits and river estuaries along the entire NSR. Thus, the Arctic Group of Forces (AGF) was charged not simply with defending territory but also with protecting Russia's economic interests in the region. In turn, this could require increasing the strike capabilities of the Northern Fleet which was (and is) seen as an important instrument for demonstrating Russia's sovereign rights in the High North and protecting its economic interests in the region.

Although the document was mostly designed for the domestic needs (particularly, it aimed at setting priorities for the AZRF development) many foreign analysts tended to interpret the Strategy-2008 as a 'solid evidence' of Russia's revisionist aspirations in the region (Huebert 2010; Schepp and Traufetter 2009; Willett 2009). For them, the Russian plans to 'define the outer border of the AZRF', create the AGF and build a network of border guard stations along the coastline of the Arctic Ocean were the best proofs of Moscow's expansionism in the region. The Kremlin's mantras on a purely defensive nature of these initiatives were taken with a great skepticism.

The National Security Strategy of the Russian Federation through 2020, released in May 2009, also underlined the quest for energy resources, which are considered to be the potential means for Russia to remain a great power. The document confirmed

Russia's interest in the North, which was elevated to the status of the Caspian Sea and Central Asia as one of the main energy battlegrounds of the future (Medvedev 2009).

Strategy-2013. Since the Strategy-2008 was of a rather general nature it should be specified and regular updated by other documents. On February 20, 2013, the Strategy for the Development of the Arctic Zone of the Russian Federation (Putin 2013) was approved by President Vladimir Putin, which revised and updated Strategy-2008. It should be noted that this document does not fully reflect Russia's Arctic doctrine, as it covers only the AZRF rather than the whole Arctic region. In this sense, it is comparable to the Canadian and Norwegian strategies for the development of their northern territories.

Strategy-2013 has some international dimensions, including, for example, Moscow's intention to legally delimit Russia's continental shelf in the Arctic Ocean and file a new application to the UNCLCS, as well as its emphasis on the need for international cooperation in areas such as the exploration and exploitation of natural resources, environmental protection, preservation of indigenous people's traditional economy and culture, etc. However, the main objective of the document is, first and foremost, to provide a doctrinal/conceptual basis for the AZRF's sustainable development, i.e. it is designed for domestic rather than international consumption.

Reactions to Strategy-2013 have varied in the Russian and international expert community. To its credit, Strategy-2013 is much more realistic (even pessimistic in some cases) than Strategy-2008. In fact, it acknowledges that the main objectives of the previous strategy were not achieved in the first phase of 2008–2010 and should be reformulated for the future. For instance, it tasks all actors involved with crafting a federal program for the sustainable socioeconomic development of the AZRF and completing all the preparatory work to launch it by 2015, not 2010 as the old strategy required. Moreover, the document acknowledges that Russia lacks the necessary resources and technologies to exploit the AZRF's natural resources on its own and needs foreign investment and high-tech assistance to develop its Far North. The new strategy also reflects the fact that Russia was unable to complete geophysical research on the external limits of Russia's continental shelf by 2010 (as required by Strategy-2008) and sets the more realistic goal of completing this work by 2015.

Strategy-2013 is naturally more detailed than Strategy-2008, as it was explicitly designed to elaborate and build on the earlier strategy. For example, it contains a crude SWOT analysis of the AZRF and a rather detailed list of policy priorities, as well as a description of the mechanisms and instruments to be used in the course of executing the strategy.

It also introduces the long-awaited idea of making the AZRF a separate federal entity with its own monitoring system, reflecting the specifics of the AZRF and the need to deal with the region on an individual basis.

Unlike the previous document, Strategy-2013 envisions an important role for regional and local governments as well as private business (public-private partnerships). The document describes in detail how to engage both regional and local governments and business in ambitious Arctic projects.

Strategy-2013 also pays much more attention to environmental problems in the Arctic. The document establishes a set of priorities for Russian environmental policies in the AZRF and pledges a significant financial contribution to future environmental projects in the region.

A clear advantage of the new strategy is its effort to introduce an indicator system of monitoring socioeconomic and security developments in the AZRF. The Strategy-2008 was rather abstract and declaratory in nature, and was essentially devoid of specific parameters or indices.

The Strategy-2013 has a more detailed description of the military aspects of Moscow's policies in the Arctic. Particularly, the document sets up the following tasks in the military/national security sphere:

- Ensuring a favorable operative regime for the Russian troops deployed in the AZRF to adequately meet military dangers and threats to Russia's national security.
- Providing the AGF with military training and combat readiness to protect Russian interests in its EEZ and deter potential threats to and aggression against the country.
- Improving the AGF's structure and composition, providing these forces with modern armaments and infrastructure.
- Improving air and maritime space monitoring systems.
- Applying dual-use technologies to ensure both AZRF's military security and sustainable socio-economic development.
- Completing hydrographic works to define more precisely the external boundaries of Russia's territorial waters, EEZ and continental shelf (Putin 2013).

It is also noteworthy that Russia's new AZRF strategy is much more open to international cooperation in the interests of solving the numerous problems in the Arctic and ensuring the sustainable development of the region as a whole. Like its predecessor, Strategy-2013 emphasizes Russia's sovereignty over the AZRF and NSR, and calls for the defense of the country's national interests in the area. However, coupled with this rather traditional stance is an impressive list of priority areas for cooperation with potential international partners. As a result, Strategy-2013 received a more positive international reception than the previous document.

But Strategy-2013 has also met with criticisms. To begin with, it does not clearly define the AZRF, which is unusual for this type of document and stands in contrast to both Strategy-2008 and the draft of the new Russian AZRF strategy, which was originally designed by the expert organization North-Western Strategic Partnership (NWSP 2011). Whether the authors of Strategy-2013 decided to skip the definition because it was already introduced in the 2008 version, or whether they did not define the AZRF's domestic and international boundaries because they wanted a free hand in this delicate sphere is open to debate.[4]

The terminology is equally vague with regard to how Arctic actors are defined. The document uses the terms "priarkticheskie" (literally sub-Arctic) and "pribrezhnye" (coastal) states to denote the key Arctic players. While there is no confusion about the concept of a coastal state, "priarkticheskie" is less clear. Is it simply synonymous with coastal states (as we learned from Strategy-2008), or does it mean the eight permanent members of the Arctic Council (five coastal states + Finland, Iceland and Sweden)? If only the Arctic-5 are meant, the three remaining Arctic countries might be offended by Russia's word choice.

In contrast with Strategy-2008, Strategy-2013 does not describe Russia's national interests in the AZRF. In light of the special Russian Security Council meeting on protecting the national interests of the Russian Federation in the Arctic (September 17, 2008), the new doctrine was expected to improve and elaborate on Strategy-2008's section on national interests, which was rather vague and fragmentary. However, Strategy-2013 only periodically invokes Russia's national interests in the Arctic without specifying or systemically describing them.

As noted, the document begins with a crude SWOT analysis of the AZRF. However, in contrast with the NWSP draft which contained a proper SWOT analysis in its final version, Strategy-2013 lists only AZRF's weak points and risks rather than its competitive advantages. As a result, one wonders whether the AZRF has any strong points at all.

Some priorities and specific projects mentioned in Strategy-2013 are not in line with other Arctic states' policies. For example, Moscow's intention to solve the AZRF's energy problems by building a series of floating nuclear power stations contradicts EU plans to move away from nuclear power and has alarmed environmentalists concerned about fragile Arctic ecosystems.

---

4   The presidential decree on the limits of AZRF was issued in May 2014 (Putin 2014).

It is unclear why Strategy-2013 classifies the need to complete hydrographic work to define the AZRF's external borders as a matter of military security (clause 18e). Normally, such work is intended to designate the limits of an EEZ, not for military purposes.

The idea to introduce an indicator system to monitor various aspects of the AZRF's development is a good one. But it lacks consistency and some of the indicators mentioned are strange or even irrelevant. For example, what is the benefit of counting the number of maritime research expeditions in the AZRF or the share of modern weaponry in the military equipment deployed in this area? Such a technocratic/instrumentalist approach is hardly helpful in developing an efficient monitoring system in the AZRF.

To sum up, the Strategy-2013 is a good invitation to further discussions on Russia's policies in the North rather than a comprehensive and sound doctrine. To become an efficient national strategy in the region it should be further clarified, specified and instrumentalized in a series of federal laws, regulations and task programs. The Russian Northern strategy should be also better designed for the international consumption. Despite the fact that the new Russian doctrine clearly addresses the soft security problematique, the foreign audiences—by the virtue of inertia—continue to perceive that kind of Russian documents as manifestations of Moscow's expansionist plans in the North. For this reason, the future Russian doctrinal documents should not start from the Cold War-type threat and risk analysis that implies that the country operates in the hostile international environment. On the contrary, such documents should emphasize the opportunities for international cooperation and Russia's readiness to collaborate with other regional players. Probably Russia should suggest a special program for international cooperation in the North (separate from the AZRF developmental strategy) where the Kremlin could explain in detail Russia's national interests in the region and its strategic vision of the North, including the specific priorities for international cooperation.

In April 2014, the Russian government has approved a state program on 'Socio-Economic Development of the Arctic Zone of the Russian Federation for the Period up to 2020' which aimed at the implementation of specific projects in the AZRF (The Government of the Russian Federation 2014).

Chapter 4.
The Russian Arctic: in Search of a Sustainable Development Strategy.

According to both the Russian political leadership and expert community, a sustainable development strategy (SDS) should become a key element of Russia's national policy in the region. However, it remains unclear what specifically the Russian decision-makers and academics mean under the SDS concept? How is this concept reflected in Russia's current national strategies for the AZRF? Whether the SDS has been already operationalized in Russia's concrete programs, projects and implementation mechanisms in the region or it is still—more or less—remaining on paper? The analysis below addresses these research questions.

The problem of definition

In the Russian scholarship, sustainable development is an eclectic concept, as a wide array of views fall under its umbrella. Its definition dates back to the 1987 UN Brundtland report, which defines sustainable development as 'development which meets the needs of the present without compromising the ability of future generations to meet their own needs (United Nations 1987).

The Russian experts differ by their interpretation of the SDS concept.

One school, the 'economists', following the Brundtland report's approach believes that sustainable development is a pattern of resource use that aims to meet human needs while preserving the environment so that these needs can be met not only in the present, but also for future generations. For this school, sustainable development is an economy in equilibrium with basic ecological support systems. As for the AZRF the 'economists' insist on the need to preserve its fragile ecological balance while exploring and developing region's natural resources. They oppose an unlimited economic growth and call for a mandatory ecological expertise of all developmental projects (Dobretsov and Pokhilenko 2010; Kochemasov et al. 2009; Kontorovich et al. 2010).

The 'green', environmentalist, school makes emphasis on the ecological aspects of the SDS. The 'greens' believe that the Arctic ecosystem is unique and—at the same time—fragile. For this reason, it cannot be sacrificed to the AZRF's successful economic development based on the exploitation of natural resources (Dushkova and Evseev 2011; Ekologicheskoe Sostoyanie Impactnykh Raionov 2012). The environmentalists criticize Russia' official Arctic strategy that aims at making the AZRF a 'strategic resource base'. They underline that the AZRF should avoid the 'resource curse' and keep its ecosystems intact. They warn that if the economic activities in the Arctic would not be reduced to the reasonable minimum the ecological implications will be catastrophic not only for the region but also for the entire world. They note, for example, that the Arctic shapes not only the regional but also the world weather.

The third, 'anthropological'/human-centric, approach focuses on the social aspects of the SDS underlining the necessity to subordinate its economic and ecological components to the needs of human development. For this reason, the main attention is paid to the 'human dimension' of Russia's Arctic strategy—indigenous peoples, urban population, labor migrants, etc. (Fomina 2013; Savel'eva and Savel'ev 2010).

However, over the last decade the so-called integrated approach to the SDS that has been proposed by both the UN and Arctic Council (AC) gained a momentum in the Russian academic community [Heininen, Sergunin and Yarovoy 2014]. According to such an integrated approach, the SDS is conceptually broken into three constituent parts: environmental, economic and social (see figure 2).

Figure 2. Sustainable development: three dimensions

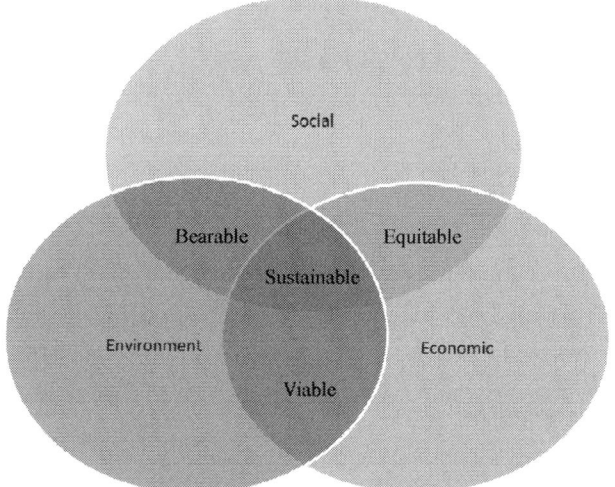

In principle the Russian expert community shares the AC integrated approach to the SDS in the High North and it has the following priorities for the AZRF:

Economic dimension of sustainable development

- Sustainable economic activity and increasing prosperity of Arctic communities,
- Sustainable use of natural, including living, resources,
- Development of transport infrastructure (including aviation, marine and surface transport), information technologies and modern telecommunications.

Environmental dimension of sustainable development

- Monitoring and assessment of the state of the environment in the Arctic
- Prevention and elimination of environmental pollution in the Arctic.
- Arctic marine environment protection.
- Biodiversity conservation in the Arctic.
- Climate change impact assessment in the Arctic.

- Prevention and elimination of ecological emergencies in the Arctic, including those relating to climate change.

Social dimension of sustainable development
- Health of the people living and working in the Arctic,
- Education and cultural heritage,
- Prosperity and capacity building for children and the youth.
- Gender equality.
- Enhancing well being, eradication of poverty among Arctic people

The Russian version of the SDS in the Arctic is better explained by the Russian expert assessments of the global climate change's implications for the region.

Climate change's implications for the AZRF

Both Russian policymakers and academics acknowledge the manifold effects of climate change on society, the economy and international relations in the Arctic region. Along with environmental and societal implications, climate change contributes to the existing instability in the Arctic region, and may lead to disputes over trade routes, maritime zones and previously inaccessible resources. This competition could pose security threats to particular countries of the region and contribute to international instability.

Moscow is aware of the fact that, in contrast with Antarctica, the Arctic region lacks a proper international legal regime to cope with security threats and challenges, including environmental ones. The Arctic-5 (the five Arctic coastal states—Canada, Denmark/Greenland, Norway, Russia, and the United States) deliberately seek to avoid signing any binding agreement on regional security so as not to encumber themselves in the unfolding geopolitical race for the division of the Arctic continental shelf. The absence of a legal regime impedes international cooperation on soft security issues (economic, environmental an societal problems, etc.) in the Arctic and hampers the search for ways to adapt regional ecosystems, as well as socioeconomic and cultural institutions, to climate change. The situation is complicated by the interference of non-coastal Arctic states (Finland, Iceland, Sweden) and non-Arctic states (China, India, Japan, South Korea, UK, etc.) in climate change-related disputes. These states claim a legitimate right to contribute to regional environmental cooperation, as climate change in the Arctic has global implications and affects them directly or indirectly in many ways. Moreover, they have a lot to offer their international partners. Many of them have considerable experience in polar research and some (like China, Japan and South Korea) have money to invest both in Arctic research and the regional economy. It is also important to remember that the Arctic Climate Impacts Assessment (2004), the first comprehensive study on the impacts of climate change in the Arctic region, was carried out under the auspices of the AC, of which all eight Arctic states are members.

Non-Arctic states also believe that the Arctic is an asset that belongs to all of humanity, and, hence, its natural resources and transport routes can and should be exploited by all the countries of the world. The Arctic should be maximally "internationalized" (opened to international access and cooperation) and the coastal states should ratchet down their national egoism with regard to the High North, while respecting the Arctic-5's legitimate rights in the region, including their EEZs.

As underscored by Russian experts, the environmental effects of climate change in the Arctic have caused changes in human behavior, socioeconomic development and international relations. The areas where climate change poses both challenges and opportunities include fisheries, production of hydrocarbons, transport systems, tourism, and national security.

Fisheries. Russian specialists argue that climate change has the potential to increase the productivity of some fish stocks and change the geographical distributions of others. New areas may become attractive for fishing due to the increased access allowed by reduced sea ice coverage. There is not yet an international conservation and management regime in place for some waters of the Arctic high seas, which could lead to unregulated commercial fishing and related disputes.

For example, fisheries have become a bone of contention in the Russian-Norwegian bilateral relations [Heininen, Sergunin and Yarovoy 2014] Particularly, the Russian fishing lobby opposed the 2010 Russian-Norwegian treaty on delimiting maritime zones, believing that the division of zones is more beneficial for Norwegian fishers. The benefits of climate change for commercial fishing in the Norwegian "part" of the Barents Sea have also prompted Oslo to push for revision of the 1920 Paris Treaty on Spitsbergen (Svalbard), which establishes an international regime for economic activities on the archipelago. Russia and other signatories oppose Norway's calls for revision. There have been repeated clashes between Russian trawlers fishing around the Svalbard and the Norwegian coast guard, which tried to arrest them.

Hydrocarbons. Retreating ice opens up new commercial opportunities for gas and petroleum production—both onshore and offshore. This could increase competition between the five coastal states for control over continental shelf and maritime zones, as well as cause conflicts between the Arctic-5 and non-coastal states (Finland, Iceland, Sweden) and non-Arctic countries (UK, China, Japan, South Korea, India, etc.) who would like to participate in the exploitation of Arctic natural resources. The role of international agreements (especially UNCLOS—UN Convention on the Law of the Sea) and bodies (UNCLCS) are particularly important in this regard.

Transport. Retreating ice opens up new opportunities for shipping as well, including more intensive use of the NSR. This may increase competition between coastal and non-coastal states for the control of these passages and highlight the need for new legal regimes as well as transport and search/rescue infrastructure. China, Japan and South Korea (the nations that are most interested in using this sea route) insist that the NSR is humankind's asset, or commons, and should be internationalized and made available for everyone.

Russia, on the other hand, believes that it has a priority in this area for reasons of geographic proximity and history. Moscow plans to develop the NSR and create there a more advanced infrastructure.

Tourism. Russia, for instance, uses some of its icebreakers to take tourists to the North Pole from Murmansk, and needs additional infrastructure and security to accommodate tourist ships. Given the potential of climate change to expand opportunities in the tourism/recreation industry in the Arctic, both Russia and international organizations should continue to support sustainable Arctic tourism, and welcome efforts to minimize its impact on the environment. Environmental protection and benefits to local coastal communities should be primary considerations.

Migration. Climate change promises to increase migration by indigenous populations due to radical restructuring of the economy and traditional ways of life, and by the workforce in the gas/petroleum industry and the transport and military sectors. These developments will necessitate large-scale socioeconomic programs to help local populations adapt to these radical changes.

Militarization. Increasing competition for trade routes, maritime zones and natural resources continues to drive a military build-up in certain coastal states and the intensification of NATO military activities in the region. In contrast with the Cold War era, when the global confrontation between the superpowers or military blocs defined military decision-making, the current military efforts by Arctic states are about protecting economic interests and asserting national sovereignty over maritime zones and trade routes. These developments will have an extremely negative impact on international security in the region. Many Russian experts advocate for special arms control measures for the Arctic and new legal mechanisms to solve climate change-related conflicts.

International cooperation and governance. Moscow recognizes the challenge posed by climate change and included it in its Arctic strategy. Russia has called for improvements to the UN Framework Convention on Climate Change and the continuation of the Arctic Climate Impact Assessment project, which was jointly implemented by the AC and the International Arctic Science Committee.

Moscow also realizes that there is still a long way to go to create an efficient multilateral system of governance to both adapt the region to climate change and prevent related conflicts between various international players in the Arctic.

The Russian (Soviet) SDS concept (in its environmental form) dates back to 1987 Mikhail Gorbachev's speech. That speech led to various environmental initiatives, such as Finland's 1989 initiative on Arctic environmental protection cooperation, which resulted in a number of technical and scientific reports between 1989 and 1991. This ultimately led to the development of the Arctic Environment Protection Strategy (AEPS) in 1991 (Heininen 2004, 208–209).

Russia signed and ratified the most important international agreements on environment protection: the UN Convention on the Law of the Sea (1982); Convention on biodiversity (1992); International Convention for the Regulation of Whaling (1946); Fish Stocks Agreement (1995); The UNESCO Convention Concerning the Protection of the World Cultural and Natural Heritage (1972); Convention on the Conservation of Migratory Species of Wild Animals (1979); Convention on International Trade in Endangered Species of Wild Fauna and Flora (1973); Convention on the Prevention of Marine Pollution by Dumping of Waste and Other Matters (1972); International Convention on Oil Pollution Preparedness, Response and Cooperation (1990); Agreement on Cooperation on Marine Oil Pollution Preparedness and Response in the Arctic (2013); International Maritime Organization (IMO) Polar Code and amendments to International Convention for the Safety of Life at Sea (SOLAS) (Nov. 1, 2014).

The Russian national legislation on environment protection includes the following legal acts: Federal Law on Environment Protection (2002); Water Code of the Russian Federation (2006); Federal Law on Internal Marine Waters and Territorial Sea (1998); Federal Law on the Continental Shelf (1995); Federal Law on Fauna (1995); Russian Federal Law on the Ratification of the

Convention on Biodiversity (1995) and Federal Law on the Northern Sea Route (2012). This legislation constitutes an integral part of the international governance system in the Arctic region.

The Barents Euro-Arctic Council (BEAC) and the AC have emerged as the main international forums to discuss and solve Arctic environmental problems. The BEAC approved the "Barents Environmental Hot Spot List" in 2010 based on a report by the Nordic Environment Finance Corporation (NEFCO) and the AC's 2003 Arctic Monitoring and Assessment Program (AMAP). The list included 42 "hot spots" in the Barents Region, all of them situated in the Russian part of the Barents Euro-Arctic Region (BEAR) (BEAC 2011). In 2013, the eight-step process to eliminate the hot spots began with the financial support of the Barents Hot Spots Facility, which is managed by NEFCO on behalf of the governments of Finland, Iceland, Norway and Sweden (NEFCO 2013).

At the national level, a program to clean up the Franz Joseph Land Archipelago was launched by the Russian government in 2011. According to then Prime Minister Vladimir Putin, the government allocated 2.3 billion rubles (approximately USD 77 million) to the program to clear the archipelago of barrels of waste oil by 2015. Wrangel Island and Russian villages on Spitsbergen are next in line. In addition, a comprehensive analysis of the environment is planned in another seven major Arctic zones (Putin 2011). It should be noted that Russia still lacks a sound and coherent environmental strategy in the Arctic. In recognition of this, Russia's recent Arctic doctrine, Strategy-2013, calls on relevant agencies to develop one in the near future.

Conclusion

The Russian academic community has managed to develop a comprehensive vision of the Arctic SD which is based on the combination of different interpretations of sustainable development—economic, ecological and social/human.

The Russian doctrinal documents (including the most recent ones) acknowledge the need for the SD of the Arctic environment.

Numerous efforts have been made over the last two decades to solve most acute environmental problems of the AZRF, including the program of environmental clean-up on the Arctic islands.

However, the course toward a combination of modernization and innovation with SD charted by the Russian government should move from making declarations to the implementation phase involving specific, realistic and the same time environmentally friendly projects in the AZRF.

For example, some development plans are problematic from the environmental point of view and not tuned with those of neighbors. The problematic issues include development of hydrocarbon resources (Prirazlomnaya rig, Yamal LNG plant, potential oil spills, etc.); terrestrial pollution; permafrost; ecological problems pertaining to a potential increase in the NSR traffic; plans for floating nuclear stations, etc.

It should be also noted that there is no special environmental strategy/program for the AZRF (hence there is no funding/financial facility for this). The environmental SDS is often understood by the Russian policy makers and experts in a rather technocratic/instrumentalist way and reduced to the specific, uncoordinated projects (e.g., nuclear waste treatment; 'cleaning-up' the environmental mess on the Arctic islands and archipelagos—Franz Joseph, Novaya Zemlya, Svalbard, Wrangel, etc.).

There are also some NSR-related problems, such as the need to improve the Russian legislation (in line with the IMO Polar Code) and SAR/fighting oil spill capabilities.

It is also important that the Russian strategy for the SD of the Arctic environment should be based on a more solid financial basis than at the time-being.

Since the international dimension of the Russian SDS in the High North is crucial for its success, the Russian strategy in this sphere should better fit in the framework of the regional cooperation in the Arctic, including existing institutions and programs.

Chapter 5.
Paradiplomacy: a Joker?

The concept of paradiplomacy denotes parallel international activities of subnational and non-state actors that have limited capabilities—in terms of resources and legal powers – in the foreign policy sphere as compared to national governments. According to Soldatos (1990) and Duchacek (1986 and 1990) who invented the concept, paradiplomacy is a part of the processes of globalization and regionalization, under which sub- and non-state actors play an increasingly influential role in world politics. Regions, municipalities, companies, NGOs, etc., seek to promote international cooperation, and account for a significant part of contemporary cross- and transborder contacts. The phenomenon of paradiplomacy raises new theoretical questions concerning the role of the state, substate and non-state actors in international affairs as well as it challenges the existing state system and international law that has provided the grounds for the international political order in the Westphalian era (Hobbs 1994; Hocking 1993; Keating 1999).

Thus the purpose here is to examine how the Russian northern subnational actors use paradiplomacy as a resource for problem-solving in various contexts and ensuring their sustainable development. In particular we focus on the following questions: What are the basic motives laying behind the subnational actors' international activities? What strategies, instruments and institutions are available for them to implement their foreign policies? And finally: what are the implications—negative and positive—of the policies pursued for Russia's domestic and international positions and the unfolding of political space in the North more generally?

Local goes global

In the Cold War era, when the principles of the Westphalian prevailed, there was scant space for other actors other than states in the sphere of international relations. Subnational entities such as regions and municipalities were expected to remain exclusively within the sphere of the 'domestic'. However, the prerogative of states to insert divisive borders has gradually eroded and consequently various sub-state actors have been able to establish relations of their own and to do so even without any decisive supervision exercised by their respective states. Subnational actors could thereby contribute to the emergence of transnational space and in general the emergence of a more diverse and polycentric world.

As far as the Russian northern subnational actors are concerned the initial thrust for their external activities can be also explained by the harsh realities of the 1990s. In the Yeltsin era many Russian Arctic territories felt themselves as almost abandoned by the federal government; they had to seek for survival strategies of their own. Foreign aid and investment were seen as one of the most efficient instruments for keeping afloat the local economies. In fact, given a broad autonomy of the members of the Russian Federation in the Yeltsin period the northern regions managed to develop rather diverse international contacts.

However, with time, when the socio-economic situation in Russia under the Putin regime improved, subnational entities tended to see international cooperation as an integral part of their strategy of sustainability rather than a strategy of survival. This paradigmatic shift in subnational units' motivation has entailed the radical change in their attitudes to and approach vis-à-vis paradiplomacy (Joenniemi and Sergunin 2014). Arguably, the romanticism of the earlier phase has waned and in consequence, subnational actors became more pragmatic and rational as to the policies pursued. Given the scarcity of resources available and the changes in financial conditions surrounding the EU cross-border cooperation programs (Brussels introduced the 50:50 matching funds rule), collaborative projects became less ambitious and more realistic. Overall, they boiled down to the rather practical needs of those engaging in cooperation.

Thus, regions and municipalities now tend to coalescence across borders in order to solve concrete and shared problems and this is done for reasons of their own and by employing the competence that they themselves harbor. They aim at adding to their strength by transgressing various borders—be they conceptual, identity-related or spatial—and do so by joining forces in the context of various regional endeavors, or for that matter, through lobbying in various broader contexts. What used to be in the 1990s idealistically motivated and mainly citizen-driven endeavors with issues such as peace, friendship and mutual understanding high on the agenda has more recently turned into something far more mundane and elite-oriented. In essence, the driving force, one spurred by various economic, social, cultural as well as environmental concerns, amounts increasingly to that of self-interest.

This then also implies that the pursuance of paradiplomacy has become less chaotic and more prioritized. In essence, it has been subordinated to the long-term developmental strategies of subnational actors. At the same time, however, they have been compelled to take into account the various restrictive measures imposed by the Putin administration with the aim to establish a more efficient federal control over the external policies of regional and local governments. Notably, in some cases Moscow's restrictive policies have actually derailed promising international projects such as, for example, the creation of an industrial park on the Finnish-Russian border between Imatra and Svetogorsk, or establishment of the Pomor Special Economic Zone on the border between the Sør Varanger community (Norway) and Murmansk Region (Russia).

As far as other motives of paradiplomacy are concerned, some Russian regions have been interested in partaking in the federal decision-making in the sense of stating their view prior to a final decision being reached or the international treaty signed. For example, the Murmansk region wanted to be involved in preparing international agreements where its status has been affected (visa regime, delimitation of maritime spaces, establishment of special economic zones and customs regimes, etc.).

Furthermore, and importantly, the underlying logic has in many cases turned Europe-related (i.e. transnational) rather than remained state-oriented (bi-national). With some of the financial means available for the Euroregions, twinning and other forms of cooperation coming from the EU and related funds, the profile of the subnational actors involved has become quite Europe-oriented. Previously closed and barred spaces of the Russian Arctic—with regions/cities at the edge of statist space being unavoidably seen as peripheral—have been opening up as these border entities aim at benefiting from cross-border networking. It may also be observed that subnational actors have, for a variety of reasons, become part of an increasingly competitive logic, and they have been compelled to devise active strategies of their own. Crucially, they also seem to have the self-confidence required to do so and act in this context according to their own self-understanding and specific needs.

On a more general note, although the networking of subnational actors is in the first place underpinned by the logic of competition and carried by an interest in conducting a kind of local 'foreign economic policies' (Wellmann 1998: 11) the consequences of such moves reach far beyond the economic sphere. The currently ongoing "economization" of inter-regional and inter-city relations implies that these actors now basically follow a rationale of their own in linking in and networking with each other. They seem, in fact, less state-oriented and aim instead, through new forms of signification and imagining space, at bolstering their own subjectivity also in the sphere of transnational relations. Even the current tensions between European countries and Russia because of the Ukrainina crisis did avert this trend.

Paradiplomacy: strategies and methods

Two main types of paradiplomatic strategies—direct (i.e., developing external relations of their own) and indirect (influencing Russian federal foreign policies) can be identified (Joenniemi and Sergunin 2014).

Direct strategies/methods include:

- *Creating a legislative basis for paradiplomacy.* This was particularly important for subnational units in the Yeltsin era when paradiplomacy was at its infancy and called for legitimacy. The regional and city constitutions/charters and normative acts of the 1990s aimed at legitimizing foreign policy activities of substate entities. Some regional/local legislation unavoidably collided with federal law (e.g. the Karelian constitution). However, it is also to be noted that in some cases local legislation forestalled the federal one: for instance, in areas such as encouraging foreign investment and land ownership. By developing the legislative base of their own the regional elites carved out their own policies in a hope to become more independent from Moscow.

In the early Putin period, however, the regional and local legislation was streamlined and increasingly subordinated to the federal one.

- *The use of the 'treaty-making power'.* Over the two past decades, this strategy was at the center of the heated debate on the treaty-making powers of the federal center, regions (members of the Russian Federation) and municipalities. Despite Moscow's resistance, since the early 1990s many Russian border sub-state actors have concluded direct agreements with the same-type international partners. With some agreements being signed by bypassing Moscow, the inevitable outcome amounted to a conflict between the federal center and the regions. However, in the end a compromise was struck between the center and local actors by deciding that such agreements should not have a status of full-fledged international treaties (this is still considered as a federal center's prerogative), they should be concluded with the partners located at the same level and not with foreign governments. Moreover, they should be prepared in consultation with the Russian Foreign Ministry.

Overall, in the post-Soviet period, the Russian northern regions and municipalities concluded hundreds international agreements. Depending on the size, socio-economic and cultural potential the intensity of the treaty-making policies greatly varied between the subnational actors.

For example, the Arkhangelsk and Murmansk regions, which are both to be considered as relatively large (by the Arctic standards) subnational actors, have pursued rather intensive treaty-making policies. The Arkhangelsk region has concluded cooperative agreements with two Norwegian, two Finnish, one Belorussian and one Armenian provinces. Notably, this region has also been allowed to have agreements not only with foreign subnational units of the same status but also with foreign government. Thus, the Arkhangelsk region has entered into an agreement on trade, research and humanitarian cooperation with Armenia and signed another one with Norway on children and families at risk (http://apparat.gov-murman.ru/intercoop/direction/index.html). The city of Arkhangelsk has altogether 12 foreign twin partners throughout the world, including four Nordic cities—Ljusdal and Kiruna (Sweden), Oulu (Finland) and Vardø, Norway. The Murmansk region has bilateral agreements with three Norwegian, three Finnish and one Swedish provinces. Moreover, this region is a part of the Finnish-Russian intergovernmental agreement on the multilateral cooperation in the north-western Russia (http://apparat.gov-murman.ru/intercoop/direction/index.html). The city of Murmansk has eight foreign twin partners, including five Nordic cities—Akureyri (Iceland), Luleå (Sweden), Rovaniemi (Finland), Tromsø and Vadsø (Norway).

To give another example, the Pechenga district (Murmansk region) which is seen as a relatively small-scale actor has the only international agreement—with the Sør-Varanger community (Norway). The document (signed in 2008) includes the pilot project on twinning between two mining towns of Nikel and Kirkenes that are located on the Russian-Norwegian border.

Despite occasional collisions with Moscow, many regions and municipalities continue to see the involvement into quasi 'treaty-making' strategy as an effective instrument both to build their capacities and enhance domestic and international prestige.

- *Establishing representative offices in foreign countries.* To facilitate direct co-operation with foreign countries some Russian regions have set up trade and cultural missions abroad. However, since the federal law on foreign trade of 1995 has stipulated that representative offices should be funded by the regions and municipalities themselves, it appeared that few regions have been able to afford the establishing of missions abroad. For this reason, a vast majority of subnational actors prefer to rely on the federal structures, i.e. Russian embassies, consulates and trade missions, in the pursuance of their international policies.
- *Accommodating foreign consular offices and trade missions.* To maintain sustainable relations with neighboring foreign countries and facilitate travel for its citizens some Russian regions and municipalities have favored the establishing of foreign consulates and representative offices. For example, Arkhangelsk and Murmansk host Norwegian consulates while Petrozavodsk accommodates a Finnish consulate.
- *Attracting foreign investment, promoting joint projects.* A number of Russian northern regions and municipalities have succeeded in creating favorable conditions for foreign investment. For example, the Canadian companies have invested or plan to invest in the mining industries (gold and silver) in Chukotka as well as Yakutia and oil fields and renewable energy sector in the Nenets Autonomous District (http://pda.www.minr egion.ru/Arctic/552/650/1693.html). Yet another example consists of the plan to create a U.S.-Russian natural park for the protection of biodiversity in the Bering Strait region with a provisional name of *Beringia*. This project is crucial for the local economy which is heavily dependent on the fishery. The planned park could be based on the experiences of the existing ethno-natural park, established in 1993, with the same name on the Russian side of the Bering Strait (see the *Beringia* park's web-site: http://beringiapark.ru/).
- *Creating a region's positive image abroad.* In order to attract foreign investors and provide the regional/local reformist projects with national and international support the Russian northwestern subnational actors have launched a rather aggressive

public relations campaign. They have arranged exhibitions, organized so-called 'cooperation days', such as the North Calotte Peace Days between the Nordic countries and the Soviet Union/Russia, and conducted festivals together with their sister towns, taken part in international fairs and advertised themselves in the media of their partners. Regional and municipal leaders have undertaken regular and public relations-oriented foreign trips. Some regions and towns have been running bilingual periodicals and web-sites targeted at foreign audiences. The main goal of such PR campaigns has been to dismiss their image of marginal, remote and depressed areas and trade it for much more positive images pertaining to creativity, dynamic development and the pursuance of innovative policies.

- *Co-operation with international organizations.* To confirm their status of global actors many regions and cities have endeavored at developing relations with international organizations. For example, they cooperate with UNESCO, UNIDO, EU, European Congress of Municipal and Regional Governments, Council of Europe, Barents Euro-Arctic Council (BEAC) and Nordic institutions.

For some Russian Arctic subnational units such as the Arkhangelsk and Murmansk regions, Republic of Karelia and Nenets Autonomous District, it has been particularly important to cooperate with the EU in the framework of the Kolarctic program (2007–2013) with the northern provinces of Finland, Sweden and Norway as partners (Obshee prostranstvo sosedstva 2012).

It should be noted that cooperation with international organizations has been important for subnational units not only in terms of getting an additional leverage in the power struggle with Moscow but also in terms of opening up them for the world-wide processes of globalization and regionalization.

- *Increasing familiarity.* While Murmansk and Arkhangelsk enjoyed some international contacts even in the Soviet times, many other regions and towns of the Russian North were virtually behind the 'Iron Curtain' in the Cold War period. A fresh start needed and it took, for understandable reasons, some time for the various subnational actors to familiarize themselves with the less bordered neighborhood. However, the familiarization was in some cases quite quick with new and more open spaces emerging in the previously quite closed borderlands.

For example, the town of Kirkenes (northern Norway), consisting of some 7.000 inhabitants but growing, has in fact been a major meeting-point for Russian-Norwegian contacts since the 1990s on a variety of levels. The town is multicultural in the sense that in addition to a Norwegian majority, there is a Sami population in the region, a considerable number of Finnish-speakers around as well as an increasing number of Russians in the city and its vicinity. The latter group amounts to some ten per cent of the city's population (Rogova, 2008, p. 29).

As noted by Rogova (2009), also a considerable number of Russians living in the Murmansk region nowadays view the Norwegian-Russian border in terms of a shared borderland. The border has turned far less divisive not just politically and in administrative terms, but also culturally and identity-wise. Rogova (2009: 31) claims that a borderland has emerged "which is neither Russia, nor Norway to the full extent". Russians visiting Kirkenes do not have the feeling of being abroad, as also indicated by Kirkenes being named 'Kirsanovka' or 'Kirik' with connotations of a small local and nearby entity/village in the language used in the Murmansk region. Visits have become frequent for reasons of shopping or, for that matter, using the Kirkenes airport for flights abroad.

In one of its aspects, the Norwegian-Russian cross-border cooperation can draw upon the somewhat idealized legacy of the so-called Pomor trade. These coastal trade contacts, which lasted for nearly three centuries before dwindling out after the Russian revolution in 1917, were quite important for the development of the northern areas. The legacy is frequently referred to and activated with the current-day cooperation and border-crossing seen as a return to traditional constellations.

Still another memory impacting in particular the local attitudes consists of that a considerable number of German troops were stationed in the region, pursuing quite repressive policies, and it was freed by the Soviet Army in 1944. For sure, the Cold War period, with perceptions of enmity as the prevalent approach, impacted the views on Russians. The negative views have, however, gradually changed and normalized. For instance, it became a common tradition to jointly celebrate the date of the liberation of the Murmansk region and East Finnmark from the Nazi occupants in October 1944.

- *City-twinning* has turned into one of the most successful and interesting forms of cross-border cooperation. Twinning stands for shared citiness and figures as a manifestation of new urban forms. It testifies, as an aspect of regionalization, with considerable clarity that the order-producing impact of national borders is waning. Northern Europe is particularly distinct in regard to successful experimenting with twinning. In this region, twinning is one of the departures used by cities in aspiring for a distinct, visible, and favorable profile, and it is, in this sense, part and parcel of their policies of place-marketing and branding in the context of the increasingly intense and transnational regionalization.

To coordinate and institutionalize twinning activities the City Twins Association (CTA) was established in December 2006. Altogether 14 cities were associated with the CTA, including four pairs located in Northern Europe: Valka-Valga (Latvia–Estonia), Imatra-Svetogorsk (Finland-Russia), Narva-Ivangorod (Estonia-Russia) and Tornio-Haparanda (Finland-Sweden) (City Twins Association, 2010).

These pairs differ by their experiences and effectiveness. While Tornio-Haparanda can be seen as a success story; Valka-Valga and Imatra-Svetogorsk can be viewed as relatively successful pairs whereas progress is still called for in the case of Narva-Ivangorod for the two towns to be credibly categorized as twins (Joenniemi and Sergunin 2011 and 2012).

With the outbreak of the world economic crisis (2008), subsequent crisis of the Eurozone and the new round of the Schengen zone's expansion (2007) the whole twinning project in Northern Europe has seems to have stalled (with a rare exception of the Tornio-Haparanda pair). Against this background the joint Kirkenes-Nikel initiative to launch a twinning project (2008) and plans to join the CTA look as a bold attempt to revive the very idea and spirit of twinning.

Twinning is perhaps still in its infancy and often oriented towards short-term rather than the long-term perspectives but will probably get more established and stronger over time. In any case, it calls as concrete projects of de-bordering and de-territorialization for added theoretical insight as well as further empirical enquiry. Whereas the urban areas and larger cities stand out as the main engines of development also in Europe's North, city-twinning remains nonetheless of considerable symbolic and political importance in testing the fixity of identities and questioning the divisive effects of borders.

- *Euroregions.* A number of the Russian border regions and municipalities have been involved into the Euroregion projects in the 1990s and 2000s. Euroregions are in essence administrative-territorial entities. They have been coined in order to promote cross-border cooperation between neighboring local or regional authorities of different countries located along shared land or maritime borders. In fact, they constitute widely known mechanisms of cooperation between regions. For example, Karelia has participated in the Euroregio Karelia together with three Finnish neighboring provinces.

It appears in general, despite the rather successful implementation of some projects within the Euroregions framework, that the overall results remain rather modest. Moreover, quite often the Euroregions have basically been reduced to what common Russians call 'bureaucratic tourism', i.e. exchanges between regional and municipal officials. With rare exceptions, the Euroregion do not seem to promote cooperation and horizontal links at the people-to-people, company-to-company or NGO levels. In other words, the

Euroregions concept—being a potentially important tool for subregional cooperation – does not appear to work properly.

To improve Euroregions' performance the Russian and international experts have recommend to (1) to clarify the legal status of Euroregions both in the Russian national legislation and European law; (2) that Euroregions are provided with a sustainable financial basis through EU and national long-term funding schemes; (3) that they receive funding to the local/regional budgets, and that the activities of Euroregions should be highlighted and visualized, so that lobbying for recognizable projects in national and international bodies becomes much easier (Lepik, 2009; Perkmann, 2003; Sergunin, 2006).

Indirect methods boil down to:

- *Influencing the federal legislation.* The local legislation not only legitimizes the external relations of the regions and municipalities but also affects the federal legislation. For example, the Novgorod law on protection of foreign investment (1994) was later has been used by the federal parliament to draft a similar legislation. It may also be noted that the experiences of Kaliningrad accrued in the context of the special economic zone *Amber* have been quite helpful in developing the federal legislation on special economic zones (SEZ).

- *Capitalizing on national diplomacy.* Since national law envisages Russian regional and local governments' participation in international activities that concern them, subnational actors have aspired to impact federal diplomacies. For example, the Murmansk authorities assisted in 2010 the Russian Foreign Ministry in negotiating the Russian–Norwegian agreement on delimitation of maritime territories in the Barents Sea. The regional government of Murmansk assisted Russian diplomats and border guards in preparing the 2010 Russian-Norwegian agreement on the visa-free regime for the border residents.

Importantly, international cooperation between various subnational actors does not stand out as something isolated but is part and parcel of a broader Russian strategy of cooperation with Europe. To sum up, and in reality, national diplomacy and the paradiplomacy pursued on subnational level mutually reinforce and compliment rather than contradict each other.

- *Conflict prevention and resolution.* With time, Moscow has realized that regionalization can serve as an instrument for problem-solving with respect to Russia's relations with neighboring countries. For example, cooperation between Finland and Karelia has been conducive to an eventual solution of the Karelia issue, i.e. a territorial dispute concerning the ceded Karelia. The cooperative links between Murmansk and various Norwegian actors contributed to the striking of a compromise between Moscow and Oslo on the demarcation of the Barents Sea. Likewise, the Alaska-Chukotka cooperation has eased the U.S.-Russian tensions on the delimitation of the Bering Sea.

- *Exploiting the parliament.* The Russian regions have used the Federal Assembly to lobby their foreign policy interests at the federal level. The Council of the Federation (the upper chamber) made up of regional representatives stands out as the most popular vehicle for the regional lobbying. The senators quite often use their official foreign trips to find new partners for their home regions and promote them on the international arena.

- *Capitalizing upon the federal infrastructure.* In order to influence federal foreign policies, regional actors often utilize the institutional structure created by Moscow in the periphery. For example, the Russian Foreign Ministry has established a special unit of inter-regional affairs. Along with the diplomatic agency, other ministries and federal bodies such as Ministry of Industry & Commerce, Customs Committee, Federal Border Service, etc., have established offices in the regions engaged in intensive international economic and cultural co-operation. Theoretically, these agencies should co-ordinate and control regions' international contacts, although in reality they often serve as additional regions' leverages to put pressure on Moscow rather than federal centre's instruments. The problem is that they are dependent on local authorities in terms of housing, salaries, professional careers and so on. Moreover, it also appears that these agencies are more often than not staffed by the locals with close connections to the regional elites.

It may also be argued that the growing dependence of the so-called 'power structures' (armed forces, police, special services) on the subnational authorities—even under the Putin regime—cast doubts on their loyalty to the center.

- *Exploiting international organizations.* In order to pressure Moscow, regions have managed to use not only federal institutions but also to exert influence in the context of various international organizations. For instance, the northern areas of Russia have been represented at the Barents Regional Council (BRC) and consequently used this forum to develop direct ties with the neighboring regions of Finland, Norway and Sweden as well as to get a more privileged status inside the country (visa-free regime for border areas' residents, more liberal customs regime, federal funding for the development of international academic cooperation, etc.)

Furthermore, in the real life subnational units usually combine both direct and indirect methods because they are of complimentary rather than mutually exclusive nature.

The Institutional framework

Obviously, the pursuance of paradiplomacy calls for a favorable institutional setting. A proper and supportive institutional framework allows various subnational units to be both active and successful in their paradiplomatic initiatives.

As indicated by the figure 3 below, the Arctic institutional network includes several layers.

On the top, ***supranational***, level, there are institutions set up by the **EU**, the largest regional actor. For example, **European Territorial Cooperation** (ETC), previously known as INTERREG Community Initiatives, has been part of the EU policy since 1990 providing a framework for the implementation of joint actions and policy exchanges between national, regional and local actors from different member states and neighboring countries. The ETC has grown from a relatively small INTERREG program to a fully-fledged strand of the EU regional policy with its separate regulatory framework envisaged for the period 2014–2020.

In 2007–2013 the Kolarctic program was run by the CBC program of the European Neighborhood Partnership Instrument. The Kolarctic program area includes the Norwegian provinces of Nordland, Troms and Finnmark, the Swedish Norrbotten, the Finnish Lapland and three Russian subnational units—the Arkhangelsk and Murmansk regions and the Nenets Autonomous District. The Republic of Karelia and Leningrad region have been eligible for some Kolarctic-related projects as well. The Finnish province of Lapland was responsible for the administration of the program. About 50 projects related to the development of economic and transport infrastructures, logistics, small and medium-size business, innovative entrepreneurship, preservation of the indigenous peoples' economies and cultures, research and education were supported and implemented by the Kolarctic program in northern Russia (http://www.kolarcticenpi.info/ru).

As to the future of the ETC, three strands (cross-border, transnational and interregional) will be maintained in the financial period of 2014–2020. This plurality will no doubt facilitate its implementation and the use of the already gained experience.

Figure 3. Institutional network in the Arctic region

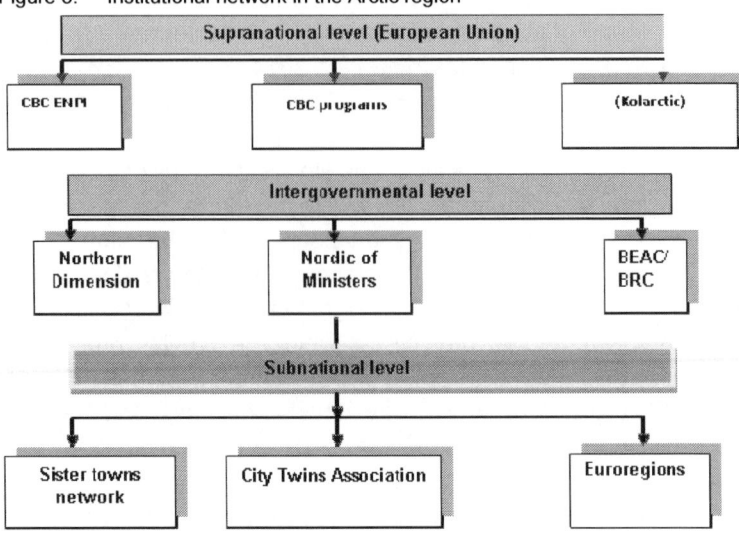

To avoid unnecessary inter-institutional duplication it is important that in the future ETC stronger emphasis will be given to the thematic concentration and strengthened links to other EU programs. However, it should be guaranteed that the themes to be presented by the European Commission as priority ones are sufficient to cover the differing needs of CBC-TBC. A delicate balance between a greater regional flexibility and the need to achieve results with scarce resources at hand has to be found. Balance, however, can be achieved only if all the parties to the negotiations are treating each other as partners.

As Hübner (2012) emphasizes, ETC should be strengthened, not only orally, but also financially. This is why the European Parliament (where various regional interests are better represented) consistently pushed for the seven per cent target in the ETC spending in all its three strands and all its dimensions, internal and external, in the multiannual financial programming period for the years 2014–2010.

The *intergovernmental* level is represented by several institutions. The **Northern Dimension** (ND) which has been transformed from the EU BSR/NE-oriented project to a system of equally-funded partnerships between the EU and three neighboring countries (Iceland, Norway and Russia) is clearly the most important one. Currently, ND includes four partnerships (on environment; transport and logistics; public health and social wellbeing; culture) which are seen as promising venues for CBC-TBC with Russia. Since 2007 (when the transformed ND was launched) dozens projects in the above areas have been implemented in various regions, including those of Kaliningrad, Karelia, Murmansk. These projects have been supported by the international financial institutions such as European Bank of Reconstruction and Development, Nordic Investment Bank and Nordic Environment Finance Corporation.

The **Nordic Council of Ministers** is yet another important regional and intergovernmental actor. According to the Guidelines for the NCM's cooperation with North-West Russia 2009–2013, Council's priority areas include: (a) education, research and innovation, including creative industries; (b) the environment, climate and energy; (c) promotion of conditions for economic co-operation and trade, including legislative co-operation, anti-corruption measures and the protection of intellectual rights and patents; (d) the ND's partnerships—especially for public health and environment; (e) promotion of democracy and civic society through co-operation on local government and good governance, co-operation between parliamentarians, co-operation between the media and journalists, and co-operation between NGOs (Nordic Council of Ministers 2009, 2–3). The NCM has several information offices in north-western Russia.

The problem with the ND partnerships and NCM is that they have a multi-focused agenda as their activities do not only cover the Barents and Arctic regions but also the Baltic Sea area. Both institutions should, it seems, avoid duplications and there is clearly a need to establish an improved division of labor between them. This is especially important in view of the scarcity of resources available to the regional actors.

In institutional terms, the NE 'flank' is covered by the Barents Euro-Arctic cooperation. Along with the inter-ministerial **BEAC** there is the **BRC** which includes 13 counties from Finland, Norway, Sweden and Russia (five of them belong to the Russian North). For example, at its Kirkenes meeting in June 2013, the BRC adopted a new *Barents Program 2014–2018* with the aim to promote creative businesses and fast growing enterprises in the region; increase CBC to achieve economies of scale and quality of life; support joint management and preservation of natural resources; implement a joint climate change adaptation; enhance innovation and research cooperation by increasing critical mass; focus on missing cross-border links in the transport infrastructure; foster mobility across the borders for workers, enterprises, tourists and students; focus on cultural cooperation in order to develop mutual understanding and regional development (The Barents Euro-Arctic Council 2013). Given the numerous overlaps with the 'sister' institutions involved at cooperation at the subnational level (ND, NCM, Arctic Council), BEAC and BRC are seeking synergy with them. These two councils have managed to install cooperation on project level with the above bodies in areas, such as climate change research and the Barents environmental hot spots elimination.

In addition to supranational and intergovernmental levels, there is also a purely **subnational** layer represented by the City Twins Association, sister towns networks and Euroregions. These organizations are rather important in encouraging paradiplomacy in the Arctic region as they operate at the subregional and municipal levels. The problem with the upper institutional levels is that they are run by the EU bodies and/or national governments, not by subnational units themselves and, for this reason, mostly aim at the macro- rather than mezo- and micro-regional levels neglecting cooperation between the EU and Russian sub-state units. In contrast with the governmentally-sponsored institutions the above fora were created by subnational units themselves, in the bottom-up way.

A proper division of labor between all these actors is called for. For example, the BRC and ETC could be especially useful in developing and implementing joint projects with Russian regions in areas such as environment protection; energy; development of local transportation, cross-border infrastructure, public-private partnerships and fund-raising for specific projects. In some spheres, such as regional transport systems; public health and quality of life; science, education and culture the ND and NCM could take a lead. The CTA is helpful in sharing best practices in urban development as well as solving common municipal problems.

To sum up, almost all the actors involved more or less clearly recognize that their task is to ensure the rightful architectural and financial demands for further cooperation in the NE.

Implications of paradiplomacy

In all, the record of the various Russian northern sub-state actors remains quite mixed as to the impacting of the policies of the federal center. On the one hand, the aspirations of sub-national actors and the center often overlapped. Their interests have been compatible in matters such as the promotion of cross-border trade, attracting foreign investment and know-how, development of cross- and trans-border transport infrastructures, facilitation of visa regime for the residents of border regions, environmental projects, tourism, youth cooperation, cultural and academic exchanges. A number of success stories as to center-periphery cooperation can be identified consisting of visa liberalization and delimitation of the Barents Sea agreements with Norway. The same can be said about the unfolding of the Karelia Euroregion and Kolarctic program as well as city-twinning in the cases of Imatra-Svetogorsk and Nikel-Kirkenes.

Yet, and on the other hand, the federal center has been quite uneasy about Russian regions and municipalities going international. Their conduct of paradiplomacy breaks with the state-centric logic of constructing political space, deviates and breaks with such logic and is therefore unavoidably conducive to worries about separatism and unwarranted external influences. At large, the reserved attitude has amounted to some distrust and, on a more concrete plane, lack of financial and administrative support to regions and cities aiming at bolstering their international contacts and cooperation. Some new city-twinning projects and Euroregions in the Russian North, have therewith been compelled to remain promises rather than concrete projects with substantial contents. They stand out as interesting as initiatives, but have not been given the chance to developed and matured into concrete projects. It may also be noted that the regional and local actors have, on a number of occasions, expressed their discontent with and mistrust in regard to the policies pursued by the center. These policies have been depicted by sub-state actors as being – at a minimum – inefficient.

In general, there is a growing feeling among the subnational actors that the very philosophy of the center-periphery relations in the field of external relations should be radically changed as the current one has proved to be quite inefficient. There is an obvious need on the federal side to improve its record if it is to cope properly with the challenges that sub-state entities are facing in the context of glocalization and in their pursuance of paradiplomacy. The federal policies should undoubtedly be better in tune and compliment rather than conflict with the policies of the subnational actors. This implies, in short, that the search for better coordination and an optimal combination of the international strategies of regional/local and central governments' international strategies is bound to continue.

Conclusion

It appears, overall, that a clear shift has taken place in the subnational units' motivation to engage in paradiplomacy. While in the Yeltsin the establishment of international contacts was a part and parcel of the survival strategy as well as an additional arm in the center-periphery tug-of-war, in the Putin and Medvedev eras it turned into a means to ensure units' sustainable development and improve their international image and attractiveness. It hence appears that the pursuance of paradiplomatic has become less anarchical and destructive, more pragmatic and skillful, better organized and coordinated with federal diplomacy. Although clashes can still be periodically identified, both sides—the centre and periphery—now tend to increasingly see paradiplomacy as a common resource rather than an area of contention.

Various Russian subnational actors have, for their part, managed to develop an arsenal of specific methods of paradiplomacy that fall into two categories—direct and indirect. The latter includes seeking legitimacy and international recognition *via* the adoption of local normative acts, signing partnership agreements, establishing representative offices abroad, attracting foreign investment, improving international image; cooperating with international organizations, city-twinning as well as partaking in Euroregions. The indirect ones pertain to measures and policies such as influencing the federal legislation, exploiting the national parliament, capitalizing on federal diplomacy and infrastructure in the regions and exploiting international organizations. Despite the division, it has been broadly viewed that the combination of the direct and indirect strategies is the best guarantee of success in the conduct of paradiplomacy.

The Russian sub-state units have managed—with Moscow's help and on some occasions without it—to exploit the institutional network that has been shaped by supranational (EU), intergovernmental (ND, NCM, CBSS, BEAC/BRC) and subnational actors and now is available at the BSR/NE. This rather dense network, however, clearly needs better coordination, organization and division of labor to eliminate bottlenecks, bureaucratic procedures, parallelisms and duplications.

As for the paradiplomacy's implications for the Russian domestic and foreign policies it can also have some negative consequences. It may under adverse conditions amount to a further disintegration of the single economic, financial, administrative and cultural space. Furthermore, it may be conducive to the rise of some rather parochial interest group as well as the emergence of self-willing and outward-oriented local elites and the outcome may amount to partial regionalization and privatization of security and military structures. The negative record can also include inconsistencies in the application of international strategies caused by the regional elites' intervening the decision-making process and even—at least theoretically – contribute to the rise of separatism and secessionism, which could result in disintegration of the country.

However, on the other hand, the gradually growing international activities of subnational actors also bring a number of positive changes. First and foremost, paradiplomacy encourages further democratization of the Russian administrative system, including managing the external relations of regions and municipalities. It has also—in being a part of the devolution process – helped to discredit the "top-down" model of the Russian federalism and encouraged a replacement with the "bottom-up" process with very lively grass-roots. Moreover, international cooperation has allowed many regions, and in particular some remote and border-located regions, not only to survive the transition period but turn their marginality into an advantage.

At large, the devolution of power that has taken place in Russia has boosted the conduct of foreign relations for the part of the subnational units. It has, in fact, facilitated their turn into some quite real international actors. It is also obvious that paradiplomacy has served as an instrument for problem-solving with respect to Russia's relations with neighboring countries and has, in this regard, an important integrative function. The reaching towards the international by numerous subnational actors has actually counteracted trends pointing to Russia's marginalization or international isolation. Moreover, paradiplomacy has been conducive to democratization and it will undoubtedly continue to play an important transformative role in Russia's future. Rather than contributing to disintegration, as has been sometimes feared, it appears to have served as a catalyst for the pursuance of successful reforms and partaking in international integration.

Chapter 6.
Northern Sea Route.

The physical and economic geography of the NSR. Moscow defines the NSR as a historically existing national unified transport route of the Russian Federation in the Arctic, and therefore considers it to be under its exclusive jurisdiction. Although Russia's Arctic coastline stretches more than 14,000 km across the Barents, White, Kara, Laptev, and East Siberian seas, the NSR is considered to lie between the Kara Gate, at the western entry of the Novaya Zemlya straits, and the Provideniya Bay, at the southern opening of the Bering Strait, for a total length of 5,600 km (see figure 4). The Barents Sea is therefore not an integral part of the NSR's legal regime. The NSR includes nearly 60 straits, the main ones being the Vilkitski, Shokalski, Dmitri Laptev and Sannikov straits, and passes through three archipelagos, Novaya Zemlya, Severnaya Zemlya and the New Siberian Islands. The legal definition is thus made more complex as there is not one single shipping channel; rather, there are multiple lanes, and the NSR crosses through waters of varying status: internal, territorial and adjacent waters, EEZ, and the open sea (Dunlap 2002; Moe and Oystein 2010; Stepanov, Orebech and Brubaker 2005). Indeed the course of the route depends upon whether the ship crosses close to the coastlines or further out, or chooses to bypass Severnaya Zemlya.

Figure 4. The water area of the Northern Sea Route (according to the Russian Federal Law of July 28, 2012).

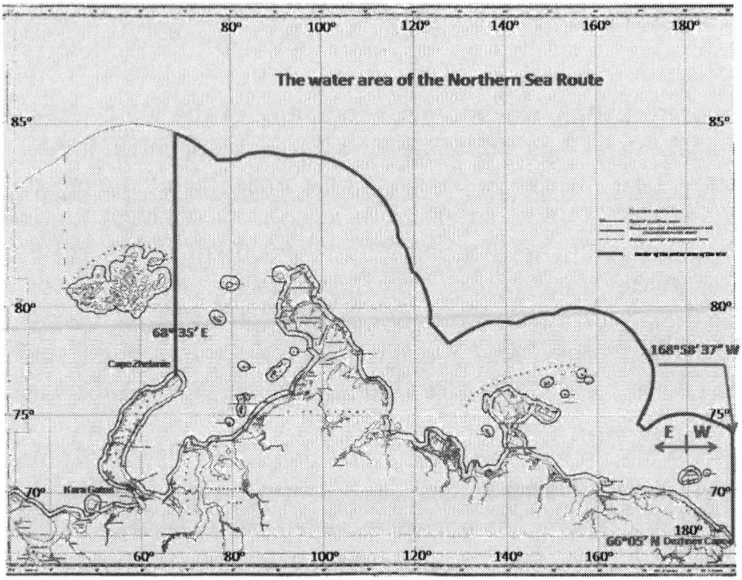

Source: http://asmp.morflot.ru/en/granici_smp/

The NSR has been vitally important to Russia both economically and socially since the Soviet era. The NSR is now actively used by such companies as Norilsk Nickel, Lukoil, Gazprom, Rosneft, Rosshelf, and Novatek to ship products and supplies to and from their plants, mines, oil and gas fields. It is also one of the main routes for Russia's "Northern supply" which delivers foodstuffs, consumer goods and fuel to the northernmost Russian settlements.

In the Soviet era, the NSR was solely a domestic sea route and was closed to international shipping. However, as Arctic ice continues to melt, the NSR will become more accessible for navigation. Today, Russia has significant interest in transforming the NSR into a sea line of communication open to international trade (Dunlap 2002; Moe and Oystein 2010; Ragner 2000). The cost of maintaining an Arctic fleet, in particular icebreakers, as well as port infrastructure is extremely high, and so any additional source of revenue is welcome. As international navigation grows, the cost of intra-Russian trade will decline.

The NSR's competitive advantages. It is widely acknowledged that an ice-free Arctic could significantly reduce transportation costs by cutting the distance from Western Europe to Japan or China by 20% to 40%. All the Asian cities north of Hong Kong could reach Europe more rapidly via the Arctic than the Suez Canal.

As such, the potential benefits of opening the NSR are of greater interest to Japan, Korea and China than, for example, India. It's easy to see why. The trip between Hamburg and Yokohama using the Suez Canal is 18,350 km, compared to just 11,100 km using the NSR. This would cut sailing time from 22 to 15 days, a 40% reduction. From Rotterdam to Shanghai via the Cape of Good Hope is 22,200 km, and only 14,000 using the NSR. The volatility in the Middle East, especially since the Arab Spring of 2011, an overburdened Suez Canal, rising tensions in the Strait of Hormuz and, most importantly, growing piracy in the Horn of Africa, are all driving the search for new alternatives.

Crossing the Arctic would also shorten transit from Russia to the North American continent. Murmansk is only 9,600 km from Vancouver via the Bering Strait, but 16,000 km via the Panama Canal. In 2007, Russia and Canada both began talking about the idea of an "Arctic bridge" connecting the Port of Churchill in Manitoba to Murmansk. The idea had already been proposed some years before. OmniTRAX, a major railroad operator that owns the Port of Churchill, had been in negotiations with the Murmansk Shipping Company on the project. In 2007 and 2008, the first shipments of Russian fertilizer from Kaliningrad to the Farmers of North America cooperative of Saskatoon arrived in Churchill from Murmansk.

The NSR's weaknesses. In contrast with the optimistic expectations discussed above, some international experts point out that travel along the NSR poses a number of significant challenges (Antrim 2010; Laruelle 2014, 176–181; Moe and Oystein 2010; Smith and Giles 2007; Stepanov, Orebech and Brubaker 2005).

First, the disappearance of polar ice during the summer does not mean that the Arctic Ocean will ever become totally ice-free. Ice can quickly form in a wide variety of locations and can take ships by surprise, reducing the predictability of travel. There will still be icebergs, and the danger of collision will remain considerable.

Second, travelling in an extreme climate and darkness during the Polar Night poses technical challenges and requires ice-class vessels, including ice-breaking capacities.

Third, there are numerous administrative technical barriers to be taken into account, such as the Russian demands that foreign ships pay to charter icebreakers, access weather and ice reports, and hire Russian pilots to guide vessels in the straits. These costs are considered too high by the main international shipping companies.

Fourth, insurance tends to be very expensive, as international insurance companies have to take into account the NSR's unpredictability both in terms of shipping times and conditions.

Fifth, the NSR currently has a limited operational rescue system, with only three rescue centers in Dikson, Tiksi and Pevek. The number of deep-water ports that are able to host ships in need of repairs is insufficient given the considerable risk of collisions stemming from unpredictable ice conditions and the lack of clearly defined lanes of direction. The Russian government plans to build 10 search and rescue centers along its Arctic coastline (see http://www.arctic-lio.com/nsr_searchandrescue), but it remains an open question whether these plans will ever be realized and whether these centers are sufficient to bring the NSR up to the level of international safety standards.

Sixth, maritime traffic in the Arctic region will increase the risk of accidents, which pose an environmental hazard. The recent international agreement on preventing and fighting oil spills in the Arctic signed at the AC ministerial meeting in Kiruna (May 15, 2013) is a helpful step in the effort to address environmental threats but still insufficient to solve the problem.

Seventh, China, the most important potential user of the NSR has recently changed its priorities with regard to the future plans to develop its transport routes from East Asia to Europe. In 2013 Beijing announced its ambitious plans to develop a New Silk Road from China to Europe *via* Central Asia which will consist of land routes (highways and railroads) with some branches *via* the southern parts of the Russian Siberia and Urals. The 'maritime component' of the New Silk Road will be based on the southern sea routes (*via* the Suez channel) rather than on the NSR (Humpert 2013). While the idea to use the NSR is not totally abandoned by Beijing it is obvious that now this route is of limited interest for China.

Eighth, a number of geopolitical and geoeconomic factors, such as the downfall of trade between Russia and Europe after the introduction of the EU sanctions and Russian countersanctions in 2014 and the drop in oil prices that made oil production in the Arctic unprofitable, reduced the interest of other (than China) potential customers from Europe and East Asia to use the NSR.

These concerns, however, do not preclude both Russia and potential NSR users from building new plans to develop this important Arctic route.

Russia's policies on the NSR. Moscow first offered to open the NSR to international shipping as early as 1967, with the beginning of détente between the superpowers, but the idea didn't go anywhere. Mikhail Gorbachev repeated the offer in his Murmansk speech (1987). The route was formally opened to international use in 1991, just a few months before the collapse of the Soviet Union. The rules for using the route were established in the Regulations for Navigation on the Seaways of the NSR (1991), the Guide for Navigation through the NSR, the Regulations for the Design, Equipment and Supply of Vessels Navigating the NSR (1995), the Federal Law on the NSR (2012) and the Ministry of Transport's Rules of Navigation through the NSR (2013).

The latter two documents stipulate conditions of transit and impose new insurance requirements, under which responsibility for possible environmental damage and pollution lies with ship owners, and which set rather costly tariffs for assistance and logistical information. Icebreaker assistance, sailing master services, radio communication and hydrographic information are provided by the federal state unitary enterprises Atomflot (nuclear icebreakers, pilot services) and Rosmorport (diesel icebreakers) as well as by private companies such as the Far Eastern Shipping Company, Murmansk Shipping Company, the Murmansk transport branch of Norilsk Nickel, Lukoil (diesel icebreakers) and Ice Pilots Ltd (pilot services). The NSR Administration, which was revived in March 2013, considers applications to navigate the NSR, coordinates the activities of the above companies and oversees navigation safety.

The binding rules released by Russia's Ministry of Transport have been accepted by major international insurance companies. However, the U.S. rejects them, believing that acceptance of such regulations would mean recognizing Russia's sovereignty beyond its territorial waters. The International Chamber of Commerce has expressed concerns, arguing that the UNCLOS regime on straits used for international navigation should take precedence over the rights of coastal states. Moreover, the U.S. argues that under the regulations only foreign ships have to pay for possible environmental damage and pollution, while Russian ships are exempt. Moscow denies that the regulations are discriminatory, noting that all ships—Russian and foreign—must present civil liability and insurance certificates when applying to use the NSR (The Northern Sea Route Administration 2013).

Legal disputes aside, since 2009 international shipping companies have started consistently using the NSR. The peak of traffic was in 2013 when the NSR Administration received 701 applications from Russian and foreign companies (http://asmp.morf lot.ru/en/perechen_zayavlenii/), 620 of them were approved (http://asmp.morflot.ru/en/razresheniya/) and 81 were declined (http://asmp.morflot.ru/en/otkazu/). The same sources estimate that freight traffic through the NSR exceeded one million metric tons in 2013 (Ol'shevski 2013). Since 2014 there was a decline in the NSR traffic: 661 applications were received by the regulatory body (http://asmp.morflot.ru/ru/perechen_zayavlenii/2014/) and 30 of them were denied (http://asmp.morflot.ru/ru/otkazu/2014/). By July 2015 368 applications were received by the NSR Administration (http://asmp.morflot.ru/ru/perechen_zayavlenii/) and two of them were declined (http://asmp.morflot.ru/ru/otkazu/).

Contrary to Western assumptions, almost all rejected applications were declined on purely technical grounds, such as incomplete information on the ships listed on the application or lack of proper documentation. In fact, more applications from Russian vessels were rejected than from the foreign ones. In 2013 the ratio was 63:18; 2014 presented a slight deviation—14:16; in 2015 only two Russian applications were rejected (http://asmp.morflot.ru/en/otkazu/). There was the only "political case" in the NSR Administration's practice over the recent years when the application from the *Green Peace* icebreaker *Arctic Sunrise* was rejected four times in 2013. Three denials were based on the lack of information on technical details (such as the class of the vessel or its ice belt breadth), and the fourth denial was based on the ship's violation of the Regulations on Navigation through the NSR: "Navigation in the water area of the Northern Sea Route from 24.08.2013 to 27.08.2013 without permission of the Northern Sea Route Administration, as well as actions taken that created a threat of marine pollution in the water area of the Northern Sea Route, which is covered in ice for most of the year" (http://asmp.morflot.ru/files/zayavka/20130920143952ref%20A%20S.pdf).

As part of its effort to internationalize the NSR, Moscow has launched a number of investment projects to upgrade the route's infrastructure. To this end in 2012–2014 over 21 billion rubles are allocated for the construction and modernization of maritime infrastructure in the Arctic.[8] Some experts expect the volume of freight traffic in both Eastern and Western directions of the NSR to reach 35–40 million metric tons per year by 2020,[9] while others continue to have serious doubts about not only the prospects of the NSR as an alternative route to southern ones but also about the need for infrastructure development in the High North. These analysts believe that Russia has more important priorities, such as developing the national transportation system.

Despite some legal inconsistencies surrounding the NSR and the lack of proper infrastructure, it will remain a priority of Russia's strategy in the Arctic region going forward. The Kremlin considers the NSR an effective resource for developing the AZRF both domestically and internationally. For this reason, Moscow plans to make considerable investments in the NSR and bring its infrastructure in line with international standards.

However, as with other aspects of its Arctic policy, Russia faces a difficult dilemma: how to maintain control over the NSR while also opening it up to international cooperation and integration with the global transportation system.

Chapter 7.
Russia's Relations with Major Arctic Players.

This chapter addresses Russia's policies towards key Arctic powers, as well as the most important supranational actors, NATO and the European Union. Russia's relations with the main Arctic actors consist of four major "circles": (1) the coastal states, including Canada, Denmark, Norway, Russia, and the United States (the Arctic-5); (2) three sub-Arctic countries (the rest of the Arctic-8: Finland, Iceland and Sweden); (3) non-Arctic states (East Asian countries such as China, Japan and South Korea), and (4) international organizations and forums dealing with Arctic issues (primarily the UN, Arctic Council, Barents-Euro-Arctic Council, Nordic institutions, European Union and NATO) (see figure 5).

Figure 5. The structure of Russia's relations with regional actors

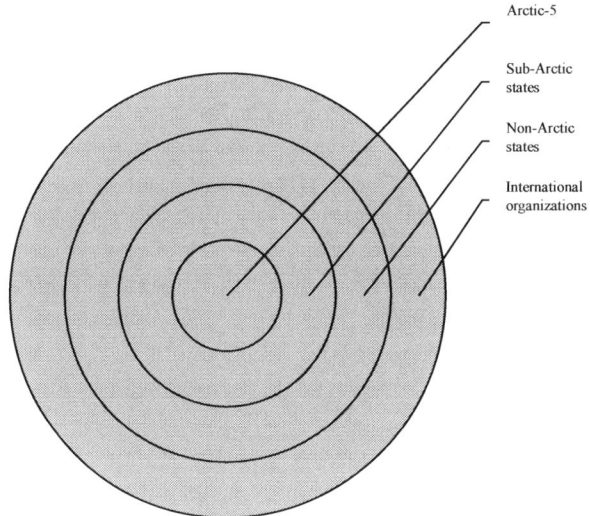

U.S.-Russia

With increased competition for the natural resources of the High North and the need to establish a proper Arctic governance system, it is important for Russia to build a policy of cooperation with such an influential regional and global player as the U.S. Given the U.S. geopolitical and geoeconomic potential and authority it is clear that none of the most important questions of the Arctic can be solved without Washington. Is there any potential for cooperation between the U.S. and Russia in the High North? Or is the U.S. focused on pursuing a unilateral course of action in the region?

What does the Arctic mean for the U.S.? The U.S. is represented in the Arctic by the State of Alaska, its only northern territory, whose continental shelf contains about 31% of the undiscovered oil reserves in the entire Arctic, or 27 billion barrels. Gas is also expected to be found there but in much smaller quantities (U.S. Geological Survey 2008). 20% of American oil and 8% of silver are produced in Alaska. This state provides 10% of the world zinc production. The Bering Sea and adjacent waters provide for a half of the U.S. fish catch.

Based on recent U.S. Arctic doctrines (National Strategy for the Arctic Region 2013; U.S. Department of Defense 2013), American interests in the region can be divided into several groups. First, it has military-strategic interests, including missile defense and early warning systems; deployment of sea and air systems for strategic sealift; strategic deterrence; maritime presence and maritime security operations; and ensuring freedom of navigation and overflight. Washington is prepared to act unilaterally if necessary in defense of these interests.

Second, the U.S. has a national security interest in preventing terrorist attacks or other criminal acts that increase its vulnerability in the Arctic region.

Third, the United States has political and economic interests—above all, expanding its presence and activity in the region to bolster its sea power. While remaining within the limits of its jurisdiction in the Arctic, Washington intends to do more than just protect its sovereign rights in its EEZ and exercise "appropriate control" over the contiguous waters; maintaining freedom of trans-Arctic overflights and freedom of navigation throughout the Arctic—including the NSR which is seen by Russia as a zone under its jurisdiction—have also been declared top national priorities.

It should be noted that Washington's motivation in the Far North has significantly changed over the post-Cold War era. During the Cold War, the Arctic was predominantly an area of military and strategic confrontation with the Soviet Union, whereas now economic interests—access to oil and gas resources in the Arctic—are the primary goal.

Between rivalry and cooperation. There are both overt and concealed differences between the U.S. and Russia on the Arctic issues. Like many other countries, the U.S seeks to define the status of the NSR, running along the Arctic coast of Russia, as international. However, this would not only cost Russia significant revenue from the use of the route by other countries, it would increase Russia's military and strategic vulnerability from the north. Moreover, Moscow believes that shipping through the NSR without the Russian icebreaker and pilot escort can increase the risk of shipwreck and oil spills. For these reasons, Moscow rejects the U.S. favorite principle of freedom of navigation with regard to the NSR saying that this is a unique case and Russia feels herself responsible for maritime safety and environment protection in this water area.

Moscow and Washington also see the leading regional institution, the Arctic Council, differently. Russia is interested in expanding the AC powers, while the U.S. considers the Council only a forum for discussion and opposes granting it the status of an international organization with the authority to make binding decisions. As the U.S. Arctic Council presidency program for 2015–2017 demonstrates, Washington has no plans to reform this institution and intends to limit the AC's role to the discussions on environment protection, climate change mitigation, maritime safety, etc. (U.S. Department of State 2015).

The U.S. also strongly supports strengthening NATO's presence in the Arctic in a bid to push out other international/regional organizations, such as the AC and the BEAC (in which the U.S. is not a member). Given the current state of relations between Russia and NATO, this would have negative consequences for Russia, which has no reliable allies in the Arctic.

Until the U.S. ratifies the UN Convention on the Law of the Sea, there remains the possibility of worsening disputes with Russia over borders in Arctic seas and over the continental shelf boundary. The U.S. has already demonstrated that it opposes Russia's attempts to expand its continental shelf to the Lomonosov and Mendeleev Ridges. Russia's application to the UNCLCS was rejected in 2001 due to the U.S. State Department pressure. Russia has not ratified the treaty with the U.S. on the Bering Sea boundary line (see section on territorial disputes).

Despite these tensions, U.S.-Russian relations have significant potential for cooperation in the Arctic. These relations are based on the Ilulissat Declaration signed by the "Arctic five" in May 2008, which recognizes the Convention on the Law of the Sea of 1982 as the legal basis for drawing borders, and states that the parties intend to resolve problems through negotiations. In keeping with Barack Obama's stated desire to reset relations with Russia, there were statements, including by the president himself and the secretary of state, on U.S. intentions to cooperate with Russia in the Arctic. However, it is likely that cooperation will be limited to those areas where the U.S. cannot do without Russian participation, particularly SAR operations in the Arctic, which was addressed in an international agreement signed under the auspices of the Arctic Council in May 2011.

There are also plans for large-scale cooperation to develop the natural resources of the AZRF. In April 2012 Russia's Rosneft and the U.S. company Exxon-Mobil signed an agreement on cooperation in the exploration and development of oil and gas deposits in the Kara Sea. Russia benefited from this arrangement by attracting the necessary financial resources (Exxon-Mobil has a capitalization of $400 billion) and modern technologies for exploration and drilling in northern latitudes. Rosneft and ConocoPhillips, an American multinational energy corporation, were also developing the promising Ardalinskoye field in the Nenets Autonomous Area.

Unfortunately, with the introduction of Western sanctions against Russia in 2014 the above-mentioned companies had to suspend their exploration activities in the AZRF. According to some media reports, Exxon-Mobil lost $1 billion because of the cancellation of projects in the Kara Sea (Nilsen 2015).

Another opportunity for bilateral cooperation is the development of circumpolar air routes, which involves building and maintaining communications infrastructure, as well as upgrading existing airports in Russia and building new ones.

Cooperation between the U.S. and Russia in the field of Arctic research and environment protection remains mutually beneficial. Obviously, any decisions relating to the economic development of the Far North should be based on scientific analysis of the vulnerability of northern ecosystems and the difficult weather, social, domestic and other conditions. Russia has a fleet of icebreakers to contribute and enormous experience with Arctic expeditions.

In the military-political sphere, the two parties should pursue confidence and security building measures (CSBM) in the region. Such CSBMs could include advance warning of deployments of naval forces in "sensitive" zones, as well as limiting the U.S. and Russian military presence in the Arctic.

At present, it is difficult to predict how relations between the U.S. and Russia in the Arctic will evolve. This will depend, first, on the general mood in Russian-American relations, which is susceptible to change in the domestic situation in one or both countries or international crisis. For example, the ongoing Ukrainian crisis has caused a general decline in U.S.-Russian bilateral relations and led the U.S. to unilaterally suspend cooperation with Russia in several areas, including hydrocarbon exploration, military-to-military contacts and CSBMs development.

Second, it will depend on the success of Russia's economic policy in the Arctic, which seeks to attract foreign investment and technology. Some positive steps have already been taken in this regard.

Third, it will depend on whether the U.S. sticks to its present course of predominantly unilateral action in the region (reiterated by recent U.S. national security and military doctrines), or opts for multilateral cooperation instead.

Canada-Russia

The Canadian sector of the Arctic is the second largest (25%) after the Russian sector (40%), and Canada is one of five coastal Arctic states that—in accordance with international law—have preferences in economic activity on the Arctic shelf.

Canada's interests in the Arctic. Canada's main interest in the Arctic is to exploit its vast natural resources such as oil and gas. Along with conventional oil and gas deposits, the coastal area of the Canadian Arctic has huge reserves of methane hydrate. If commercial production is launched, these reserves would last for several hundred years. Nevertheless, about a third of Canada's proven oil and gas reserves are not in use yet. Safe technologies have not yet been developed, and Canada does not conduct drilling on its Arctic shelf. The mechanism for insurance coverage in the event of a major accident or a threat to the environment has not been worked out either. In addition to oil and gas resources, the Canadian North has significant reserves of valuable minerals such as diamonds, copper, zinc, mercury, gold, rare earth metals and uranium.

Another of Ottawa's priorities in the Arctic region is ensuring the sustainable socioeconomic and environmental development of the Canadian North. Should polar ice continue to melt, the Northwest Passage (NWP), over which Canada claims control, will only grow. If the NWP becomes ice-free, it could theoretically offer comparable economic benefits as the Northern Sea Route around Russia's Arctic coast, though in practice it is much more difficult and demanding to navigate. Compared to the Panama Canal, however, the NWP provides a significantly shorter route from East

Asia to Europe and the east coast of the United States and Canada. Moreover, transit fees are not imposed.

Ottawa's policy priorities in the Arctic were outlined in a document titled Canada's Northern Strategy: Our North, Our Heritage, Our Future (2009).

Territorial disputes. Along with Russia and Denmark, Canada is seeking to extend the limits of its shelf to the underwater Lomonosov Ridge by filing a request with the UNCLCS at the end of 2013. In order to demonstrate that this ridge is an extension of the North American continental shelf, a U.S.-Canadian shelf survey was conducted in 2008–2009 north of Alaska onto the Alpha-Mendeleev Ridge and eastward toward the Canadian Arctic Archipelago. Russia is preparing a similar request (the first request, filed in 2001, was unsuccessful). So, Russia and Canada are at odds on this issue.

The Lomonosov Ridge is not Ottawa's only territorial dispute with its Arctic neighbors. Canada is also challenging Denmark for ownership of the 1.3 km^2 uninhabited Hans Island, and the borderline in the Lincoln Sea. Canada is also in a dispute with the United States over the maritime border in the Beaufort Sea, which potentially has oil and gas, as well as over the status of the Northwest Passage (Canada insists on its sovereign rights to this passage, while the U.S. considers it international waters).

However, these arguments are not considered serious enough to prevent Russian cooperation with these countries, including in the military-political sphere.

Canada's increased military activity in the Arctic. In an effort to catch up in the field of Arctic military security, Ottawa has in recent years set its sights on expanding its military presence in the region. For example, it plans to build a military training center on the banks of the Northwest Passage in the town of Resolute Bay (595 km from the North Pole) and maritime infrastructure. To strengthen the capacity of the Coast Guard, the country plans to build deep-water berths (in the city of Nanisivik), a new icebreaker named *Diefenbaker,* and three patrol vessels capable of operating in ice. The latest Canadian space satellite RADARSAT-2, the joint Canadian-American system NORAD, and the intelligence signals interceptor station in the town of Ehlert (Ellesmere Island, Canadian Arctic Archipelago) will all be used to monitor Arctic territory. The forces of the Canadian Rangers were modernized and increased from 4,000 (2007) to more than 5,000 people by the end of 2013 (http://pm.gc.ca/eng/news/2013/08/21/canadian-rangers). They are largely recruited from the local indigenous populations and expected to monitor and carry out search and rescue operations in the Arctic.

In 2010, the Canadian government announced the purchase of 65 new F-35 Lightning II fighters from the U.S. for a total of $16 billion, including aircraft maintenance for twenty years. However, the purpose of these fighters in the Arctic is unclear. The F-35 is designed to perform tactical missions in support of ground operations, bombing and close air combat. However, none of the Arctic players has plans to land troops in the Canadian North, and a couple of old Russian bombers conducting mostly training flights to Canada's air border do not constitute a serious threat. According to experts from the Canadian Defense and Foreign Affairs Institute, these purchases are more likely intended as a security guarantee for the future than a response to current challenges. According to different estimates, Canada must address other crucial tasks: patrol aircraft for coast monitoring and a robust naval capacity.

These and other initiatives have led to a doubling of Canada's total military spending since late 1990s (Blunden 2009, 127).

Since 2008, Canada has been conducting regular exercises of its armed forces in the Arctic, as well as joint exercises with other countries. The stated purpose is to protect Canadian sovereignty in the Far North. Canada has no plans to invite Russia to participate in such exercises. Canada, the U.S. and Denmark are not only conducting joint exercises in the Arctic, but are also performing patrol functions and practicing rescue operations on the waters.

Nevertheless, Russian experts caution against overestimating the importance of these Canadian military preparations, which are more a demonstration of Canada's readiness to defend its economic interests and respond to "unconventional" (non-military) challenges in the region than actual preparation for a large-scale military conflict. The Canadians have neither the desire for a large-scale military conflict nor the logistical capabilities to execute one. Ottawa intends to continue relying on the United States for strategic defense, as this is the most beneficial arrangement both financially and functionally.

The influence of domestic factors on Ottawa's Arctic policy. Unfortunately, Canada's Northern Strategy is often held hostage to domestic political wrangling. Politicians in every camp know that the majority of Canadians see asserting the country's sovereign rights in the Arctic as the country's number one foreign policy priority. According to opinion polls, 40% of Canadians support taking a "hard line" on this issue. Canadian conservatives most often play the "Arctic card" in elections. For example, the campaign rhetoric of Conservative Party leader and current Prime Minister of Canada Stephen Harper is frequently anti-Russian and pro-American. Naturally, this is not conducive to improving relations between Moscow and Ottawa on Arctic issues.

The recent Ukrainian crisis (with some help from the pro-Ukrainian lobby in Canada) has touched off a strong anti-Russian campaign in Canada, especially in Canadian media. The Canadian government was the first to introduce sanctions against Russia, which had a spillover effect on Ottawa's relations with Russia in the Arctic region, temporarily freezing political dialogue between the two countries in the Arctic Council in which Canada currently presides.

Prospects of Russian-Canadian cooperation in the Arctic. Despite the fact that Russia and Canada are competitors in the process of dividing the Arctic, they adhere to some general principles that suggest that cooperation is possible even in this problematic area.

The legal basis for Russian-Canadian relations includes the Political Agreement on Consent and Cooperation of June 19, 1992, and a series of economic agreements: Promotion and Reciprocal Protection of Investments (1991); Trade and Commercial Relations (1992); Economic Cooperation (1993); Avoidance of Double Taxation and the Prevention of Fiscal Evasion with Respect to Taxes on Income and on Capital (1995); Air Communication; Principles and Bases of Cooperation Between the Federal Districts of the Russian Federation and the provinces and territories of Canada (2000); Cooperation in the Peaceful Uses of Atomic Energy (2007).

There are a number of documents that directly address Arctic issues. For example, the Joint Russian-Canadian Statement on Cooperation in the Arctic and the North, signed on December 18, 2000, outlined the main aspects of bilateral cooperation in the region. In November 2007, during a visit to Canada, the Russian prime minister signed a number of sectoral agreements on Russian-Canadian cooperation in the Arctic, the peaceful use of atomic energy, agriculture, fisheries, veterinary and phytosanitary control, and in the financial sphere.

Apart from the legal framework, the institutional framework of Russian-Canadian relations is also growing stronger. In 1995, the Russia-Canada Intergovernmental Economic Commission (IEC) was created. The IEC consists of an industrial agriculture subcommittee and working groups on construction, fuel and energy, mining, the Arctic and the North. As of today, nine IEC meetings have been held. The last regular meeting of the IEC was held on 17 June 2013 in Moscow.

In addition, the Russian-Canadian working group on cooperation in the field of climate change has been operating since September 2002 (formally outside the IEC). The Canada-Russia Business Council (CRBC) was created in October 2005. It includes working groups on agriculture, mining, energy, information and telecommunications technology, transport, finance, and the forest industry.

Despite the potential for conflict, Russia and Canada have numerous opportunities to establish Arctic cooperation in the following areas.

Trade and economic cooperation. The Northern Air Bridge project involves the creation of an integrated communications system in the Arctic (for example, by launching satellites into highly elliptical orbits and developing the necessary ground infrastructure) to ensure air communication between the airports in Krasnoyarsk and Winnipeg. Another project, Arctic Bridge, involves transpolar shipping between the ports of Murmansk and Churchill.

The largest joint investment projects in the Russian Arctic are:

- purchase and development of the Kupol and Dvoynoe gold fields in Chukotka (Kinross Gold Corporation);
- development of the Mangazeyskoe silver-polymetallic field in Yakutia (Prognoz CJSC/Silver Bear Resources);
- design and supply of equipment for the third phase of the construction of the Koryaga Oil Fields project in the Nenets Autonomous Area (Globalstroy Engineering/SNC LAVALIN);
- development of the Fedorova Tundra field (Murmansk Region);
- adopting Canadian "cold asphalt" technology in the construction of roads in the extreme climatic conditions of the Arctic (Yakutia);
- design and production of Arctic all-terrain vehicles based on air-inflated caterpillars;
- promoting the deployment of wind-diesel systems capable of operating in the Arctic conditions of the Nenets Autonomous Area, etc.

Scientific and technological cooperation. According to the Joint Russian-Canadian Statement on Cooperation in Science, Technology and Innovation, signed on June 2, 2011, the parties prioritize joint efforts in the areas of energy and energy efficiency, nanotechnology, biomedical technology, climate research and the Arctic. Given its lack of ice-breakers, special vessels for research in sea ice and reliable space-based communications systems,

Canada is interested in partnering with Russia to conduct joint research in the region. The numerous scientific and educational projects of Russia and Canada include cooperation between Canadian universities and the Northern (Arctic) Federal University in Arkhangelsk.

Environment. The IEC Arctic and North Working Group is implementing a range of projects under a program entitled "Conservation and Restoration of the Biological Diversity of Northern Territories and the Environmental Protection, Cooperation in the Field of Agriculture and Forestry."

In 2011, the Russian government decided to allocate in 2011–2013 €10 million for the Project Support Instrument (PSI) being created under the auspices of the Arctic Council. Thus, a collective fund, which will be used to eliminate sources of environmental pollution and environmental "hot spots" in the Arctic, was launched. A legally binding document on preventing and responding to oil spills in the Arctic region is being drafted under the Arctic Council. Among the Council's major new projects for the upcoming period is creating mechanisms for ecosystem management in the Arctic, integrated assessment of multilateral factors of changes occurring in the region, and trends in human development in a changing Arctic.

Indigenous peoples. In accordance with the Russian-Canadian Declaration of Cooperation in the Arctic (2000), several programs aimed at creating favorable living conditions for the indigenous peoples of the North are being implemented. One such program, Exchange of Experience in Managing Northern Territories, launched in 2011, is being carried out with the participation of the Plenipotentiary Representative of the Russian President in the Siberian Federal District and the Canadian Department of Indian Affairs and Northern Development. The Institute of Economics and Industrial Engineering (Siberian Branch of the Russian Academy of Sciences) is providing the necessary scientific support.

From 2006 to 2009, a Russian-Canadian cooperation program for the development of the North was implemented with the participation of the Canadian International Development Agency, the

Ministry of Regional Development of the Russian Federation, and a number of Russian agencies. It addressed issues concerning indigenous minorities in the North. The program was conducted in the Yamal-Nenets Autonomous Area, the Khanty-Mansi Autonomous Area, and the Khabarovsk Territory. Promoting natural resource exploitation and small business are among the program's primarily humanitarian cooperation projects.

Russia and Canada, through the IEC Arctic and North Working Group, are implementing numerous projects to create for indigenous minorities a model territory of traditional nature management, develop traditional local sports, and set up cultural exchanges between the indigenous peoples of the Russian and Canadian North.

Under the AC aegis, Russia is working to establish a public Internet archive of data about the development and culture of the Arctic ("Electronic Arctic Memory"), supporting young reindeer breeders of the North, and working with organizations of indigenous peoples to clear the area of sources of environmental pollution, among other initiatives.

Resolving territorial disputes. The prospects for resolution of the existing territorial conflicts are quite promising because the two countries share some common political and legal principles.

First, the two countries support resolving disputes through negotiations and on the basis of international law. That is how Moscow and Ottawa plan to solve their dispute over the underwater Lomonosov Ridge, which is promising for oil and gas exploration. Secondly, both countries support in principle dividing the Arctic on the basis of sectors (drawing direct longitudinal lines from the North Pole). The sector method is more favorable to both countries than the so-called median line method, which would create regions proportional to each country's coastline. Applying the sector method would significantly increase the area of the Arctic controlled by Russia and Canada. However, by signing the 2010 Norwegian-Russian agreement on maritime delimitation in the Barents Sea, Moscow has, in fact, acknowledged that the median principle is acceptable as well. Third, Russia and Canada are in favor of consolidating the status of transit sea routes in the Arctic (NSR and NWP) as internal waters, which would yield considerable economic benefits to the two countries.

Cooperation within the Arctic Council. Both countries assign a special role to the AC, created at Canada's initiative in 1996. The main goal of the two countries is to maintain the Arctic Council as the primary and most important forum for Arctic cooperation and strengthen the cooperation within the Council.

According to Moscow and Ottawa, the Arctic Council is a body where all the major problems of the Arctic region should be addressed—from environmental and transport security to protecting the rights of the indigenous Arctic minorities and cultural cooperation.

Russia and Canada proposed for many years that the Arctic Council better define the status of permanent observers for non-Arctic states and international organizations. This would both set clear limits on non-Arctic states and international organizations in the Arctic, while also confirming the priority of the five Arctic states. This is beneficial both for Russia and for Canada, which have the longest borders in the Arctic. A document to this effect was drawn up and signed at the AC Ministerial Meeting in Nuuk, Greenland, in May 2011, helping to streamline the process of granting permanent observer status to non-Arctic states and organizations. The Kiruna AC Ministerial Meeting (May 15, 2013) decided to grant permanent observer status to six non-Arctic states.

Security. Moscow and Ottawa have taken some steps toward greater cooperation in this sphere. An interdepartmental memorandum on military cooperation has been in effect since 1994, which involves visits between high-ranking military officials of the two countries. Since 2002, Canada has participated in the Global Partnership program, which resulted in the signing in 2004 of a Russia-Canada intergovernmental agreement on cooperation in the destruction of chemical weapons, dismantlement of nuclear submarines decommissioned from the Navy, and accounting, control and physical protection of nuclear materials and radioactive substances. Canada announced it was allocating one billion Canadian dollars over ten years ($100 million Canadian dollars annually) for this purpose. Most of these projects are being implemented in the Russian Subarctic.

Building on Ottawa's policy of demilitarizing the Arctic, Russia should consider Canada's initiative to ban nuclear weapons in the region. Russia has responded positively to this initiative (Moscow raised a similar idea under Mikhail Gorbachev), but has questions about the geographical scope of such a zone. Russia supports making the Arctic a nuclear-free zone, provided this would not affect the stationing of troops and the activities of the Russian Northern Fleet, two-thirds of which consists of nuclear-armed strategic submarines.

In recent years, Russian-Canadian cooperation has been growing in the field of "soft security" (new threats and challenges posed by climate change and expanding economic activity in the Arctic). Issues such as maritime safety, pollution, illegal migration, transnational organized crime and terrorism are increasingly taking center stage.

It should be noted, that Canadian-Russian security cooperation has been suspended as a result of the crisis in Ukraine. However, despite the current tensions caused by the Ukrainian crisis, there are grounds to expect Russia and Canada to intensify mutually beneficial cooperation in the Arctic.

Russia-Norway

As Russia and Norway are both littoral states of the Arctic Ocean and direct neighbors in the European Arctic, they have many overlapping interests and goals, as the Norwegian 2006 High North Strategy shows (Heininen 2011, 39–40).

The Norwegian-Russian relations were long complicated, however, by the disagreement over their maritime border, until in 2010 Norway and Russia signed a treaty on the delimitation of the maritime territories in the Barents Sea (see the chapter on territorial disputes), thus removing the most serious obstacle to bilateral cooperation.

This Russian-Norwegian Treaty on the Barents Sea did not, however, settle the question of Svalbard, which presents specific legal problems, including the huge difference in taxation levels between Norway and the archipelago. Russian companies accessing the Svalbard continental shelf should enjoy the same rights as the Norwegian companies, which would translate to taxes of less than 1% of the cost of the hydrocarbons produced. But as Russian lawyer Alexander Oreshenkov explained, "If a deposit beginning within the limits of the archipelago's territory extends beyond its territorial waters, the Russian companies will be expected to observe the norms of Norway's continental mainland petroleum legislation, whereby 78% of the earnings from hydrocarbons produced outside Norway's territorial waters will go to the Norwegian treasury as tax payments" (Oreshenkov 2010). These financial stakes are bound to be at the core of future negotiations.

The Russian presence on Spitsbergen/Svalbard remains a cause for conflict. Plans to build a fish-processing plant, which would compete with Norwegian firms, were not well received. In recent months, the Norwegian governor of Spitsbergen has taken a whole series of restrictive measures: he has expanded nature conservation zones to which access by Russian scientists and tourists is restricted or prohibited, he has required helicopters to obtain advance permission before landing, and has introduced regulations for all scientific projects to be registered in a specific database. When the Russian side responded to these measures by denying Norwegian scientists investigating biological resources in the Barents Sea access to the Russian economic zone, this was viewed as a discriminatory act.

Norway continues to object to Russian fishing around Spitsbergen. Since Norway introduced a 200-mile economic zone around the archipelago, it has regarded such fishing as poaching. Forcible arrests of Russian trawlers by the Norwegian navy have become more frequent. As Russia does not recognize the aforementioned decision by Norway and considers this area open to international economic activity, in 2004 Russia's Northern Fleet started regular patrols of the waters around Spitsbergen. Norway particularly objected to this move, viewing it as a sign of Russian imperial ambitions and of Moscow's unwillingness to cooperate with Oslo to settle territorial and economic disputes. Norway also has claims to part of the Arctic shelf, but these claims are much more modest than those of other states.

As leading energy suppliers in Europe, there is a good foundation for a strategic partnership between Russia and Norway in the exploration and production of oil and gas. The first step in this direction was made in 2008, when Russia's Gazprom, Norway's Statoil, and France's Total signed an agreement which set up the Shtokman Development AG company to develop the Shtokman gas-condensate field. Unfortunately, the final investment decision on this project has been postponed for the indefinite future.

The agreement signed on May 5, 2012 between Rosneft and Statoil on cooperation in the joint development of parts of the Russian shelf of the Barents Sea and the Sea of Okhotsk can also be regarded as a promising development in Russian-Norwegian economic relations in the Arctic. Of particular importance is the fact that the agreement opens up the possibility of Rosneft participating in the development of the Norwegian continental shelf areas of the Barents Sea and shows the intention of the Norwegian side to place orders with Russian shipyards for the construction of ice-class vessels and drilling platforms. This agreement may be regarded as a confirmation of the economic benefits Russia gained by resolving the maritime delimitation issue with Norway.

As a major supplier of mineral raw materials, especially in the Asia-Pacific region, Norway is objectively interested in expanding the possibilities of such exports through cheaper routes. This creates prerequisites for cooperation in maritime transport and in using the NSR as the shortest sea route between Europe and the Asia-Pacific region. However, this may lead to an element of competition, since Norway is equally interested in having its ports in the North used for the traffic flow, whose volume is expected to grow.

Russia-Denmark

Considered a coastal state due to Greenland, Denmark has high stakes in the Arctic. In its 2011 Arctic strategy the Kingdom of Denmark, including Denmark, Greenland and the Faroe Islands, (Ministry of Foreign Affairs of Denmark 2011) pursues the following priorities:

- ensuring that the Arctic remains peaceful, secure and safe (supremacy of international law, strengthening of maritime safety, exercise of sovereign rights);
- achieving self-sustained growth and development (using the highest standards in mining, renewable energy sources, sustainable exploitation of biological resources, knowledge-based growth and development, active involvement in international trade);
- promoting development while at the same time preserving the Arctic climate, environment and nature (extensive research of the consequences of climate change, protection of the environment and biodiversity);
- fostering international cooperation with foreign partners (searching for global solutions to global challenges, enhanced regional cooperation, safeguarding national interests on a bilateral basis).

Unfortunately, the Danish Arctic strategy envisages only rather limited possibilities for cooperation with Russia. For example, it is suggested, under the auspices of the Danish-Russian governing council, to cooperate more closely on strengthening navigation safety in Arctic waters. Additionally, enhanced cooperation with Russia could incorporate scientific collaboration, for example, on the continental shelf. It could also include the exchange of findings on economically, socially and environmentally sustainable development, as well as confidence building and studies on potential cooperation between the Danish and Russian defense, particularly in the maritime area.

It should be noted that Copenhagen takes the hardest line against Russia in term of delimiting the Arctic shelf. Denmark lays claim to part of the Arctic shelf and is trying to prove that the Lomonosov Ridge is an extension of the Greenland Plate. After the Russian expedition of 2007, Denmark (with the United States) hastened to send its own expedition to the Arctic to search for evidence in its favor. The general view, however, is that Denmark intends to solve all territorial disputes on the basis of the Ilulissat Declaration, i.e. using peaceful methods (Koptelov 2012).

Russia's relations with East Asian countries

East Asian countries interests in the Arctic are complex and involve certain economic aspects that should be emphasized above all. These are interests in natural resources, transportation and logistics. Then there are geopolitical interests closely linked with military and strategic spheres; and finally there are environmental, climatic and other scientific and research interests, both from theoretical academic viewpoints and for application purposes (for more detail, see The Arctic Yearbook 2012, Section I: Arctic Strategies, 46–109).

East Asian countries' interest in the Arctic's natural resources can be explained by at least two reasons—the relative deficit of such resources in these countries and by the abundance of the Arctic's natural resources.

The importance of the East Asian countries' transportation and logistics interests in the Arctic is steadily growing with the increase of the export potential of their economies and China's recent ranking as the top exporting state of the world (2010). East Asian leaders clearly understand the benefits of commercial transportation via the Arctic seas. The Northwest Passage is the shortest route from the Atlantic to the Pacific, and the Northern Sea Route, which goes all along the Arctic coast of Russia, can almost halve the distance between East Asian countries and Western Europe.

Moreover, the exploration of strategically important resources and the development of new sea routes in the Arctic are not only of indisputable commercial and economic value for East Asian countries, but also hold geopolitical and military and strategic importance.

Climate change and environment degradation are also priority issues for East Asian countries. They have specifically drawn the attention of the global community to these issues, stating that "the Arctic is the main region responsible for the weather in the Northern hemisphere, including the territory of China", that there might be a relation between the natural disasters in China and that the "stable increase in global temperatures and the melting of the Arctic ice play a critical role in this process" (Karlusov 2012).

Given their significant interests in the Arctic, East Asian countries pursue quite aggressive strategies in the region. This has been shown not only by the growth of bilateral contacts between East Asian countries and Arctic countries, but also by their active policies within sub-regional institutions such as the AC and the BEAC.

Russia has differed with East Asian countries on issues such:

- The internationalization of the Arctic. Moscow has opposed the leitmotif of East Asian countries' Arctic policies that the North is part of the commons, or a "human treasure" which should be exploited and preserved together;
- The internationalization of the NSR, granting East Asian countries (especially China, as Russia's "strategic partner") some special rights (or bypassing the existing routes due to ice meltdown);
- Upgrading East Asian countries' status in the Arctic Council by granting them permanent observer status (POS). The latter issue has become topical because East Asian countries and some other non-Arctic states have been putting pressure on the AC member states to consider their applications for POS. Russian (and Canadian) concerns in this regard were explained as follows: (a) East Asian countries have not sufficiently contributed to regional/ sub-regional cooperation, as required by the AC rules; (b) Their future roles in and potential contribution to the AC's activities were unclear; (c) Their upgraded status could legitimize East Asian countries' demands on their 'share of the Arctic pie' (natural resources); (d) An ex-

panded AC may be even less effective than the current AC; (e) Granting POS to even one applicant will inevitably result in the displeasure of others and unhealthy competition among them.

However, with time, Russian opposition to granting East Asian countries POS has waned because these countries promised big investments in the Russia Arctic Zone. There was also the possibility that, if neglected, East Asian countries could align with other rejected countries to establish an alternative organization that could undermine the AC's effectiveness. As a result, at the Kiruna ministerial meeting of the Arctic Council, China, Japan, South Korea, India and Singapore, together with Italy, were granted the status of (permanent) observers.

Potential areas for cooperation between East Asian countries and Russia could be investment in the AZRF mining, oil and gas industries; development of NSR infrastructure; introduction of the environmentally friendly maritime fuel; support for Arctic environment-related research; cooperation in the AC's working groups (Emergency Prevention, Preparedness and Response; Arctic Monitoring and Assessment Program Working Group; Circumpolar Biodiversity Monitoring Program of the Conservation of Arctic Flora and Fauna Working Group; Arctic Ocean Review Project of the Protection of the Arctic Marine Environment Working Group) and expert groups (the Ecosystem-Based Management Expert Group). It should be noted that in its relations with East Asian countries Moscow faces an uneasy choice between the need to maintain cooperative relations with China, its key "strategic partner", and protect its national interests in the Arctic.

NATO and Russia in the Arctic

Since 2008 NATO has tried to redefine its place in international Arctic cooperation and expand its activity in the entire High North. The alliance's most prominent representatives have made a series of statements on the Arctic; meetings and expert seminars have addressed the key issues. NATO clearly defined its priorities in the region at a conference on security prospects in the High North held in Reykjavik at the end of January 2009. In formal terms, NATO will focus on "soft" security—the ecological consequences of global warming and of human activity in the Arctic, the risks of ecological and manmade disasters, and so on.

This focus does not, however, exclude a purely military component of NATO policy, as reflected in a series of exercises conducted under the alliance's aegis. In fact, NATO has declared a new priority area: the global competition for resources. As envisioned by NATO leaders, the main factors influencing the alliance's military potential and development are "the political conditions in the world community, the operational and strategic situation, and the reserves of resources and their distribution at the global level." This view is confirmed by statements made by former NATO Secretary General Jaap de Hoop Scheffer to the effect that "NATO is set the task of consolidating its grip on regions that contain existing and prospective deposits of energy resources and routes of their transportation" (Scheffer 2009). In this regard, Scheffer has declared that NATO has a strategic interest in the Arctic. The alliance's Arctic states (the United States, Canada, Norway, Denmark and Iceland), however, disagree over where to draw the 200-mile boundary and the shelf boundaries; these disputes can be viewed as justification for broadening the EEZs. Scheffer proposed turning NATO into a forum in which these five countries could discuss their differences: "We must ensure that, as we look today at the High North, and perhaps in the future at other regions, we do not get drawn down the path of regionalization—because that is the path to fragmentation. And that is a path we must avoid at all costs" (Scheffer 2009).

The implication is that the Arctic states should not have sole jurisdiction over the use of the region's energy resources. To justify the alliance's military presence, Scheffer observed that certain states were expanding their military potential and activity in the Arctic. This statement may refer only to Russia, although he did not say so directly. For example, the exercises conducted in Norway on March 13–26, 2009, under the code name Cold Response, show that Scheffer's statements and NATO's involvement are aimed precisely at Russia. According to the scenario of Cold Response, "The large non-democratic state 'Nordland' has declared its rights to an oil deposit located in the territorial waters of the small democratic state 'Midland.'" However, the entry of Midland's allies into the war leads to victory. Russian experts believe that the exercises were conducted to ascertain Norway/NATO positions in the Arctic. According to a representative of the Norwegian Defense Ministry, the authors of the scenario had in mind not only Spitsbergen/Svalbard but any other territory where a dispute could arise (Diatlikovich and Grebtsov 2009).

The Russian experts disagree over the reasons and motives underlying NATO's involvement in the High North. According to one view, NATO, sensing challenges from other international organizations dealing with European, trans-Atlantic, and global security (the UN, the EU, the Organization for Security and Cooperation in Europe, the Council of the Baltic Sea States, the BEAC, the African Union, the Collective Security Treaty Organization, the Shanghai Cooperation Organization, etc.), is trying to uphold its role as chief guarantor of regional and global security and thereby prove that it is needed and effective in a changing world (Shaparov 2013).

This claim has become increasingly questionable. NATO is trying to demonstrate that, while it still has the potential to deter any military threat, it is actively transforming itself into an organization with new peacekeeping tasks: dealing with the consequences of natural and manmade disasters, search and rescue operations, the fight against illegal migration and drug trafficking, and other challenges to "soft" security. NATO plans to focus on precisely such problems in the Arctic.

Another school paints NATO as an instrument by which individual states strive to advance their own interests in the Arctic, rather than the vehicle of a united policy for the Western community (Konyshev and Sergunin 2012). For example, Norway, which assigns the High North a leading place in its domestic and foreign policy, has long called for strengthening NATO's role in the Arctic.

Speaking at the Oslo Military Society in January 2009, Norway's defense minister spoke of his country's intention to call NATO's attention to questions of the High North and observed that the alliance is now showing heightened interest in the region. Norwegian officials and independent experts point out that on its own, Oslo cannot defend its economic and military-strategic interests in the Arctic or create the necessary military potential.

Similar considerations also guide some of the other NATO member states in the unfolding "battle" for the Arctic—Canada and Denmark, for example. Like Norway, they are not in a position to stand up to more powerful rivals on their own. On the one hand, they hope that NATO will defend their interests in the face of Russia's growing strength in the region; on the other hand, they hope that NATO will arbitrate disputes over Arctic issues among its member-states and restrain increasing pressure from the United States, which has lagged behind other countries in joining the contest for Arctic resources. The United States, conversely, hopes to use its authority in NATO to exert pressure on its competitors within the alliance.

On the whole, there are many Russian decision-makers and experts who expect that NATO will continue to expand its activities in the Arctic. This may have some negative implications for Russia. Moscow is especially concerned with the NATO plans to involve Finland and Sweden into its activities and eventually incorporate them into the alliance. Particularly, the Kremlin refers to the September 2014 NATO summit's decision to enhance its military cooperation with Helsinki and Stockholm. If these two countries should join NATO, the Russian analysts warn, this could change radically the Arctic strategic balance and bring the region on the brink of a renewed military confrontation.

Opponents of this view believe that NATO is unlikely to conduct an effective policy in the region. First, it has limited scope and resources for rapidly creating the necessary infrastructure (especially amid the global economic crisis). Second, the alliance is itself driven by internal discord on matters concerning the Arctic. A number of NATO member-states have their own ambitions and claims on this region, which has led to U.S.–Canadian and Danish–Canadian conflicts over specific Arctic policy issues (definition of EEZs, division of the continental shelf, etc.). This school calls for taking into account the fact that NATO has been transformed from a transatlantic military organization for collective defense into a more global military-political institution, as its activities in the Balkans, Afghanistan and Libya show. Part of the price for this is that NATO has not so far been able to redefine its mission in the Arctic, though there have been some efforts in the early 21st century to do so (Heininen, Sergunin, Yarovoy 2014).

If, however, NATO succeeds to expand its activity in the Arctic, particularly in the European Arctic, there is a risk that NATO could try to sideline Russia in the emerging Arctic security system, as it does, for example, in the rest of Europe. Some NATO member states, such as Norway and Denmark, will continue to use the alliance to strengthen their positions in the region *vis-a-vis* Russia. In any case, Russia has therefore to prepare itself for an uneasy dialogue with NATO so as to find acceptable forms of cooperation in the Arctic.

EU, Russia and the Arctic

Since the late 1990s, the EU has shown a great interest in the Arctic, justifying this by its concern over the competition between various powers for the natural resources of the High North, over territorial disputes and the claims of several countries to control the Arctic sea passages, and over ecological "hot spots" in the region.

Initially, the EU mostly limited its activities in the Arctic to the implementation of the Northern Dimension program (for more details see Heininen 2001; Joenniemi and Sergunin 2003; Konyshev and Sergunin 2012). In the early 2000s, the idea of an "Arctic window" grew popular in the EU and was reflected in the new concept of the ND adopted in November 2006. The EU actively cooperated with three regional institutions concerned with Arctic issues—the AC, BEAC and the Nordic Council of Ministers (NCM).

In October 2007, the European Commission adopted the Action Plan for an Integrated Maritime Policy, which touched on issues such as the division of the continental shelf and the exploitation of sea routes in the Arctic.

In March 2008 the European Commission and the High Representative of the EU for Common Foreign and Security Policy (CFSP) drafted a joint document titled "Climate Change and International Security" (Commission of the European Communities 2008a) which focused largely on ecological problems. In particular, the following issues were highlighted: the destruction of the established ecosystem as a result of the melting polar ice; the negative consequences of economic activity in connection with the development of the region's natural resources and the increasing number of international trade routes; and intensified competition among Arctic powers for the use of natural resources and sea routes in the Arctic.

To prevent dangerous developments, it was proposed:

- to intensify the activity of regional organizations under the aegis of the renewed ND;
- to work out an EU Arctic strategy with special emphasis on ensuring equal access for various countries to the natural resources and trade routes of the region;
- to establish a dialogue with Arctic countries that do not belong to the EU on how global climate change might affect international security.

The non-EU (Russian, Norwegian, Icelandic, U.S. and Canadian) experts have viewed this document as a EU's attempt to claim a role in the Arctic affairs. It has also been noted that much of the impetus pushing the EU toward a more aggressive Arctic policy has come from three Arctic member-states—Denmark, Sweden, and, in particular, Finland (Heininen 2011, 26 and 29), that felt excluded from Arctic affairs despite heavily impacting and having significant interests in the region.

In November 2008 the European Commission released a communication on "The European Union and the Arctic Region,"

(Commission of the European Communities 2008b) designed to outline the key points of the EU's Arctic strategy. The document sets goals and makes recommendations for the organization of Arctic research and working with indigenous peoples, fishing, the extraction of hydrocarbons, navigation, political and legal structures, and interaction with regional organizations. In particular, it identifies the three main priorities for the EU's future policy in the region:

- protecting the Arctic environment and indigenous peoples;
- ensuring the stable development of the region and the rational use of its natural resources;
- developing a mechanism for multilateral cooperation in the Arctic.

The last point deserves special attention. The press release issued by the European Commission on the adoption of the communication states: "Enhancing the European Union's contribution to Arctic cooperation will open new perspectives in our relations with the Arctic states. The EU is ready to work with them to increase stability, to enhance Arctic multilateral governance through the existing legal frameworks as well as to keep the right balance between the priority goal of preserving the environment and the need for sustainable use of natural resources, including hydrocarbons" (The Arctic Merits the European Union's Attention 2008). The document notes the need for broad dialogue on questions of Arctic policy on the basis of the UN Convention on the Law of the Sea, and the key roles played by the Northern Dimension and the Arctic Council (in whose work Russia takes an active part) in cooperation in the Arctic.

Despite such "multilateralist" rhetoric, these documents hardly mentioned Russia and the BEAC, which are considered important regional players indispensable for the success of regional cooperation in the Arctic.

One year later, in 2009, the EU Council of Ministers of Foreign Affairs approved the Commission's communication. In January 2011, the European Parliament called for a more active EU Arctic policy, but its voice in such matters is merely advisory. Finally, in July 2012, the Commission and the EU's High Representative for CFSP submitted a progress report and an evaluation of the EU Arctic Policy (European Commission and EU High Representative 2012).

These documents may seem ambitious only if one does not take into account the above mentioned limited political instruments available to the EU. In practice it all boils down to monitoring, research and discussions, many of which are designed to persuade the Arctic countries of the need to maintain higher environmental standards, even to the detriment of their economic activity. It is not surprising that a few of the non-EU countries of the Arctic region are not overly enthusiastic about these claims although they perceive them as reasonable and do not refuse to participate in dialogue initiated by the EU. To demonstrate a relative EU's weakness in Arctic politics it should be mentioned that the Brussels' bid for the POS was declined by the 2013 AC Kiruna meeting.

It is possible to conclude that for the foreseeable future the EU will attempt to strengthen its presence in the region with increasing vigor and uphold its claims for the Arctic more resolutely. However, unlike NATO or the U.S., the EU will do this without any particular emphasis on military power, preferring to use diplomatic and economic methods.

Chapter 8.
Russia and the Territorial Disputes in the High North

The territorial disputes in the High North are seen by Russian strategists as a significant threat to the country's security. It should be noted that the Arctic region has inherited a number of territorial disputes from the Cold War era and Russia was a party to them. Some of these conflicts were successfully settled down while others are still waiting for their resolution. The analysis below addresses four cases—the U.S.-Soviet/Russian dispute on the Bering Sea, Norwegian-Russian dispute on the Barents Sea, Svalbard issue and the Russian claim on the extension of its continental shelf in the Arctic Ocean.

The U.S.-Russian dispute on the Bering Sea

Named for the Danish-born Russian explorer Vitus Bering, the Bering Sea is an 885,000 nautical mile^2 (2,292,150 km^2) extension of the Pacific Ocean that lies between Russia and Alaska. It is bordered to the South by the Aleutian Islands, and the northern Bering Strait separates it from the Arctic Ocean. It is the third largest sea in the world. The combination of its natural characteristics, such as shallow continental shelves and seasonal ice, has created one of the richest fisheries in the world. The sea is connected to the Arctic Ocean by the Bering Strait, which separates Asia from North America and is believed to have been a land bridge during the Ice Age that enabled migration from Asia to North America.

The Sources of the Dispute. There were three major causes of the conflict:

- The Bering Sea constitutes a strategically important area for both the U.S. and Russian fishing industries. It supplies a third of Russia's and a half of the United States' total annual catch (Conley & Kraut 2010). On the Russian side, commercial fisheries catch approximately $600 million worth of seafood annually, while the U.S. Bering Sea catches are $1 billion worth approximately each year (The International Bering Sea Forum 2006). Both for the Alaskan and Russian Far East's regional economies, fishery is important in terms of revenues, employment and sustainable development. For example, in case of Russia the fishing industry directly employs over 100,000 people and around one million indirectly (Laruelle 2014: Ch. 7). The Bering Sea catch is important not only for the U.S. and Russian domestic seafood consumption but also for the two fishing industries' expansion on the East Asian markets.

It should be noted that along with the legal market a quickly developing black market of Alaska pollack and Bering crab exists in the region, one which involves not only the Russian Far East but also China, Japan and South Korea. It is estimated that the fish caught in Russian waters exceeds the official quota by at least 150% (The International Bering Sea Forum 2006). This is because poaching is rampant, and the Russian organized crime is heavily involved in the fish trade. The Russian "fish, crab and caviar mafias" not only aim at expanding its commercial activities and sidelining their foreign rivals but also at establishing control over the regional governments and federal agencies in the Russian Far East.

Overfishing creates numerous ecological problems in the region. According to some accounts, as a result of intensive trawling, species such as crab and perch are in serious decline in the entire Bering Sea, while the stocks of pollack fluctuate in an unpredictable manner from year to year. The once-plentiful pollack have had especially dramatic declines on the Western (Russian) side of the Bering Sea because of illegal fishing. In the Eastern (U.S.) Bering Sea, harvests of snow crab have declined by 85% since 1999 (The International Bering Sea Forum 2006).

In turn, the ecological problems serve as another source of the U.S.-Russia tensions because they increase competition between American and Russian fishermen and lead to mutual accusations of inability to effectively regulate commercial fisheries in the region.

- The 'hydrocarbon factor' also plays some role in keeping the dispute alive. First, oil and gas deposits have been discovered in both the offshore and onshore territories near the Bering Sea. But the main 'apple of discord' is not the Bering Sea itself but the adjacent Chukchi and East Siberian Seas (parts of the Arctic Ocean) where the U.S. and Russian maritime and continental shelves' boundaries are not settled. According to the recent U.S. Minerals Management Service's estimates, the potential oil and gas reserves in the Bering and Chukchi Seas comprise some 24 billion barrels of oil and 126 trillion cubic feet of natural gas (Kaczynski 2007: 2).

- Moreover, the Bering Sea is an important transport junction between the Russian Far East and East Asia, on the one hand, and Alaska, on the other. Additionally, with growing importance of the NSR (controlled by Russia) and North-West Passage (controlled by Canada) the Bering Sea (and especially the Bering Strait) constitutes an important transit area for the future traffic from East Asia to Europe and North America (and back).

The Historical Dynamics of the Conflict. Historically, the roots of the dispute can be detected as early as in the Russo-American accord on the cession of Alaska. The Convention of 1867 determined two geographical lines—one in the Bering Sea and the second one in the Arctic Ocean—to delimit American and Russian territories. However, in case of the Bering Sea the 1867 Agreement actually only applied to maritime territories and was not intended for the delimitation of EEZs or continental shelf, the concepts that did not exist at that time.

Being concerned about the possible discovery of unknown lands by Western countries in the Arctic Ocean and repeated U.S. claims on some islands in this ocean (such as Wrangell, Herald, Bennett, Jeannette, and Henrietta Islands), the Bolshevik Russia tried to fix its control over the remote northern territories. On April 15, 1926, the Central Executive Committee of the Soviet Union issued a decree entitled "On the Proclamation of Lands and Islands Located in the Arctic Ocean as Territory of the USSR". According to the decree, the Western boundary of the Soviet sector was defined as the meridian 168°49' 30" W. long. From Greenwich, bisecting the strait separating the Ratmanov and Kruzenstern Islands, of the Diomede group in the Bering Sea (The Central Executive Committee of the Soviet Union 1964).

As some U.S. legal experts believe, in practical terms, this decree led to establishing the Soviet control not only over the five islands in the Arctic Ocean but also on the Copper Island (with Sea Lion Rock and Sea Otter Rock) which, according to this school, should belong to the U.S. under the 1867 Convention (Olson et al. 1998). However, as the U.S. State Department's official document emphasizes, none of the islands or rocks above were included in the U.S. purchase of Alaska from Russia in 1867, and they have never been claimed by the U.S., although Americans were involved in the discovery and exploration of some of them (U.S. Department of State 2009).

Over time, and in particular when in 1976 both the USSR and U.S. decided to define the limits of their EEZs in the economically important region, the 1867 Convention line in the Bering Sea became the contentious marine boundary between the two countries. In 1977 the U.S. and USSR exchanged diplomatic notes indicating their intent "to respect the line set forth in the 1867 Convention" as the limit to each countries' fisheries jurisdiction where the 200 nautical mile boundaries overlapped. However, the differences in each country's interpretation of the 1867 Convention became apparent very soon, making an area of nearly 15,000 nautical miles^2 a subject of a dispute. While the two countries agreed to continue respecting each other's interpretation of the Alaska purchase agreement as an interim measure, the U.S.-Soviet talks began in the early 1980s to resolve the differing interpretations. Unfortunately, the language of the 1867 Convention was silent on the type of line, map projection and horizontal datum used to describe this boundary. Moreover, neither Moscow nor Washington has produced the authenticated maps used during the negotiations to resolve the issue.

Figure 6. Differences Between the Bering Sea U.S.-Russian Marine Boundary of 1867 Using Rhomb and Geodetic Lines on a Mercator Projection

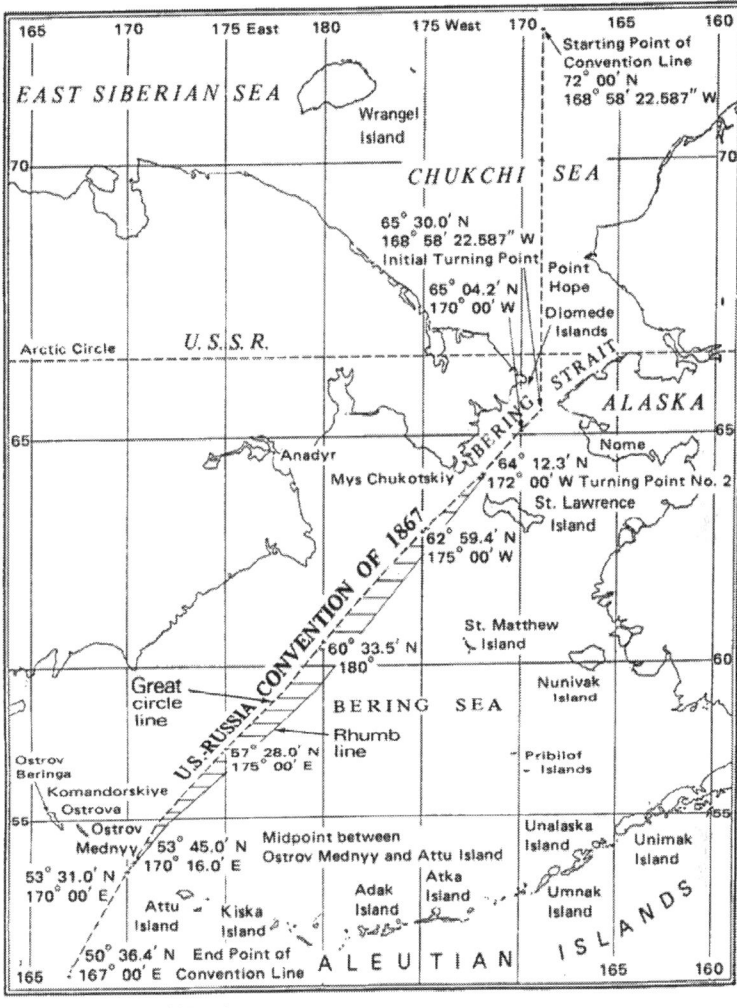

Source: Kaczynski 2007: 3

It should be noted that cartographers normally use two types of lines to demarcate marine boundaries. There are rhomb lines, on the one hand, and geodetic lines (also known as great circle arcs), on the other (Kaczynski 2007: 2). Both lines are used on two common map projections, Mercator and conical. Depending on the type of line and map projection used, lines will be either straight or curved. For instance, a rhomb line will appear as a straight line on a Mercator projection, whereas a geodetic line will be a curved one (see figure 6).

Because both Washington and Moscow interpreted the 1867 line as a straight line, the USSR defined the Bering Sea marine boundary as a rhomb line on a Mercator projection while the U.S. opted for a geodetic line on a conical projection. As a result of these differences each country's claim included a maximal part of the disputed maritime area.

It took nine years of negotiations to conclude an agreement on a new U.S.-Soviet maritime boundary in the Bering Sea. According to some speculations, Soviet negotiators may have ceded territory in the Bering Sea to the U.S. in order to waive the U.S. objections to the Soviet proposals to divide the territory north of the Bering Strait (in the Arctic Ocean). Furthermore, Moscow probably hoped that agreement with Washington could help the USSR to accelerate its talks with Norway on their maritime boundary in the Barents Sea. Other reports suggested that Washington promised some 150,000 tons of pollack compensation in an annual quota from the U.S. side of the Bering Sea if the treaty was to be signed and ratified by Moscow. Such a practice has actually existed in late 1970s but the U.S. stopped it as a part of economic sanctions against the USSR after the Soviet invasion of Afghanistan in 1979. Finally, some authors speculated that the Soviet Foreign Minister Eduard Shevardnadze simply exceeded his authority by signing the maritime boundary agreement with his U.S. counterpart James Baker (Kaczynski 2007: 4; Palamar' 2009).

However, the Russian Foreign Minister Sergey Lavrov has repudiated these speculations in 2005 by saying that the draft of the treaty was endorsed by the Soviet government (Palamar' 2009).

The agreement which was signed on June 1, 1990 (Agreement between the United States of America and the Union of Soviet Socialist Republics 1990) split the difference between the US claim to a geodetic line and the Soviet claim to a rhomb line as shown on a Mercator projection (see figure 7). The section between the Russian and U.S. sectors, which lies 200 miles out from the coastlines of both countries, is known as "The Donut Hole," and is considered international waters, or a global commons. This comprises 10% of the Bering Sea. The 1990 Agreement also created several "special areas." Special areas were areas on either country's respective side of the 1867 line but beyond 200 nautical miles from the baseline. There were three such areas on the U.S. side of the marine boundary called "eastern special areas" and one on the Soviet side called the "western special area." The USSR ceded all claims to sovereign rights and jurisdiction in the eastern special areas to the U.S. and respectively Washington ceded all claims to sovereign rights and jurisdiction in the western special area to Moscow.

The same day (June 1), in a separate exchange of diplomatic notes, the two countries agreed to apply the agreement provisionally (State Department Watch 2009). This agreement took effect on June 15, 1990. Being an executive agreement, it can be rescinded at any time by either party unilaterally.

Although both countries ceded territory from their previous claims, the US still controlled a far greater amount of area in the Bering Sea than if the new agreement had been based on the equidistant line principle normally used in international boundary disputes. It was quickly ratified by the U.S. Senate (on September 16, 1991), which was eager to keep control on the area rich in fish and to begin the sale of offshore oil and gas leases.

Criticism of the 1990 Agreement. The 1990 Agreement has evoked a heavy criticism both in the Soviet and Russian parliaments for rushing the deal by the Gorbachev-Shevardnadze tandem, ceding the Russian fishing rights and other maritime benefits. Many Russian politicians and analysts called for renegotiation of the agreement. The opponents to ratification have put forward multiple arguments.

Figure 7. The U.S.-Soviet Maritime Boundary, as of 1990 Agreement

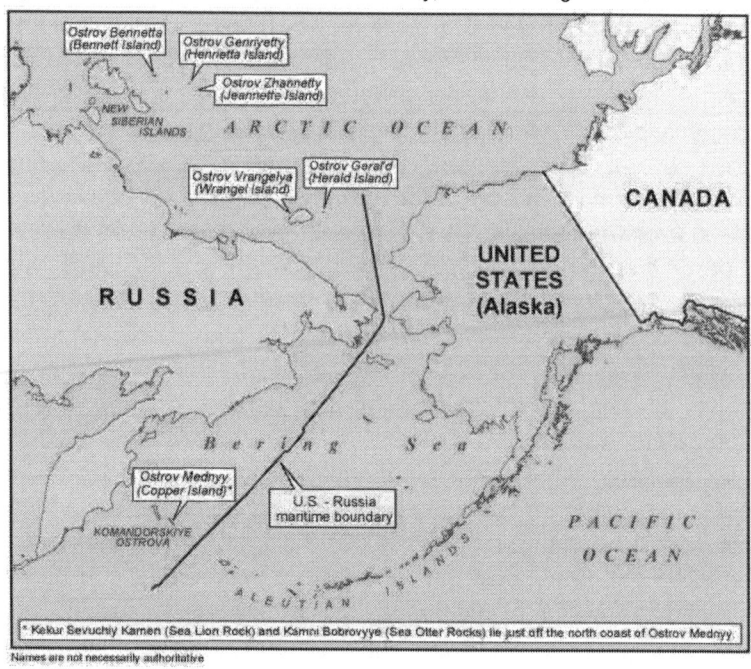

Source: http://go.usa.gov/3pBfR. Public domain.

According to one legal expert, the Baker-Shevardnadze line (which was mainly based on the 1867 Convention line) brought 70 percent of the disputed areas of the Bering Sea under American jurisdiction. If instead the median line principle had been used, it could have provided the USSR with an additional 25,000 km^2 of sea (Vylegzhanin 2010). According to the State Duma's (Russian legislature) resolution of July 14, 2002, because of the 1990 Agreement, Moscow had lost two sectors of the Soviet EEZ in the Bering Sea (23,700 km^2 and 7,700 km^2) and 43,600 km^2 of its continental shelf in the central part of the Bering Sea (beyond the 200 nautical mile EEZ). Russia has also lost between 1.6 and 1.9 million tons of fish in the 1990s (State Duma of the Russian Federation 2002). The Navarinsk and Aleut fields which are potentially rich in hydrocarbons were also ceded to the U.S.

The opponents of the Treaty have also questioned the legal status of the Baker-Shevardnadze executive agreement because the Soviet treaty law did not allow the procedure of an international agreement's 'provisional implementation' (Palamar' 2009).

As result of the above criticism first the Soviet Supreme Council and then the Russian State Duma had postponed the ratification of the 1990 Treaty for indefinite time.

There were the U.S. critics of the 1990 Agreement as well. They believed that this treaty has legitimized Russia's control over eight islands in the Arctic Ocean and Bering Sea as well as deprived Alaska from the maritime area which is rich in fish and—potentially—oil and gas.

The American opponents of the 1990 Treaty insisted that it has been concluded with numerous violations of the U.S. legal procedures. Particularly, it was prepared secretly, without consultations with the U.S. Congress. They also noted that the U.S.-Soviet executive agreement on provisional implementation of the delimitation treaty has not been disclosed in any public news release when it has been signed on June 1, 1990. It was not mentioned neither in the President George Bush's transmittal of the proposed treaty to the Senate nor at the Senate committee hearings or in the full house debate in September 1991 (Olson et al. 1998).

It should be noted, however, that in contrast with the Russian opponents to the 1990 Agreement their American 'counterparts' were marginal and unable to get significant support at the federal level (neither in Congress nor President's Administration).

Current status of the Dispute. Given the Russian dissatisfaction with the 1990 Treaty, under the Clinton administration the talks between the U.S. State Department and Russian Foreign Ministry have begun in an attempt to resolve the issue. There was even an offer to concede some fish quotas to Russia as an incentive for ratification in 1997 but it has been withdrawn by the U.S. side without any explanation (Kaczynski 2007: 5).

Washington maintains its firm position that the 1990 Treaty is binding and the Baker-Shevardnadze line constitutes the maritime boundary between the two countries. The U.S. policy aims at providing evidence of a continued "general state practice" that the boundary delineated by the 1990 Agreement is the actual marine border between the U.S. and Russia. Such evidence as well as *"opinio juris"*—a sense of obligation to comply with the practice—are required by the customary international law to legitimize an international agreement that did not fully come into force.

As some experts believe, Russia cannot legally undermine the 1990 Treaty, even if it refuses to ratify it (Laruelle 2014: ch. 5). Moscow has observed the Baker-Shevardnadze line for more than 20 years and thus helped Washington to provide both the evidence of a continued "general state practice" and *"opinio juris"*. As some Russian international law experts suggest, it is not in Moscow's interest to question the legitimacy of the 1990 Treaty because, on the one hand, such a negative policy can undermine Russia's reputation of a responsible international actor and, on the other hand, the 1867 line (on which the 1990 document is based) can be both mutually beneficial and helpful for reaching a U.S.-Russian compromise on the division of the Arctic maritime territories (Vylegzhanin 2010: 9).

As far as Russia's future policies on the 1990 Treaty is concerned Moscow can at best hope to negotiate some new, more favorable, fishing rules to compensate the losses incurred in fishing because of this agreement and create new bilateral mechanisms to open the U.S. fishing zones up to Russian fishermen. There are also some plans to create a U.S.-Russian natural park for the protection of biodiversity in the Bering Strait region with a provisional name of *Beringia* and thus to settle the problem in a friendly way (Laruelle 2014: ch. 5; Palamar' 2009). Such a park could be based on the experiences of the existing ethno-natural park with the same name on the Russian side of the Bering Strait (established in 1993) (http://beringiapark.ru/).

The two countries acknowledge the positive experiences got from the implementation of "The Convention on the Conservation and Management of Pollack Resources in the Central Bering Sea", which was signed in 1994 by China, South Korea, Russia, the U.S., Japan and Poland and was designed to regulate fisheries on the "Donut Hole."

On the formal level, the U.S. and Russia regularly holds discussions on Bering Sea issues, particularly issues related to fisheries management, but, as the American side emphasizes, these discussions do not affect the placement of the U.S.-Russia boundary or the jurisdiction over any territory or the sovereignty of any territory. The U.S. has no intention of reopening discussion of the 1990 Maritime Boundary Agreement.

The Russian-Norwegian dispute on the Barents Sea.

The Barents Sea is the part of the Arctic Ocean. Named for the Dutch explorer Willem Barents, it is bounded by the Norwegian and northwestern Russian mainland (south), the Norwegian Sea and Svalbard (west), Franz Josef Land (north), and the Kara Sea and Novaya Zemlya (east). It is 1,300 km long and 1,050 km wide and covers 1,405,000 sq km. Its average depth is 229 m, with a maximum depth of 600 m in the major Bear Island Trench.

The Sources of the Dispute. The Barents Sea is rich in various natural resources. First, due to the North Atlantic drift, it has a high biological production compared to other seas and oceans of similar latitude. The fisheries of the Barents Sea, in particular the cod fisheries, are of great importance for both Norway and Russia.

Second, according to some accounts, the Barents Sea may hold vast hydrocarbon resources. A recent assessment by the U.S. Geological Survey estimated the mean undiscovered, conventional, technically recoverable petroleum resources in the Barents Sea Shelf include 11 billion barrels of crude oil, 380 trillion cubic feet of natural gas, and two billion barrels of natural gas liquids (Klett and Gautier 2009).

Norway and the USSR started their exploration activities in the region in the late 1970s, but in the 1980s they agreed not to carry out exploration or exploitation activities in the previously disputed area. Deposits discovered so far in the Barents Sea outside the formerly disputed area include the Norwegian Snøhvit gas field and Goliat oil field and the Russian Shtokman gas field (see figure 8).

The Barents Sea is also an important transport junction between Russia, on the one hand, and North Europe and North Atlantic, on the other. Moreover, the Northern Sea Route starts on the border of the Barents and Kara seas and continues eastward.

The pursuit of control over the economically and strategically important region as well as the lack of a proper legal regime in the Barents Sea were conducive to the Norwegian-Russian dispute on these maritime territories.

History of the Dispute. The Norwegian-Russian dispute on the Barents Sea dates back to the 1920s. The above mentioned 1926 Soviet decree "On the Proclamation of Lands and Islands Located in the Arctic Ocean as Territory of the USSR" has reiterated the Tsarist Russia's legal tradition that had been characterized by the notion of the sectoral line that was, the line of longitude that starts from the terminus of the land boundary and intersects with the North Pole. The sectoral principle of demarcation of the Arctic territories, however, was not supported by some other coastal states, including Norway.

Figure 8. Oil and gas resources in the Barents Sea

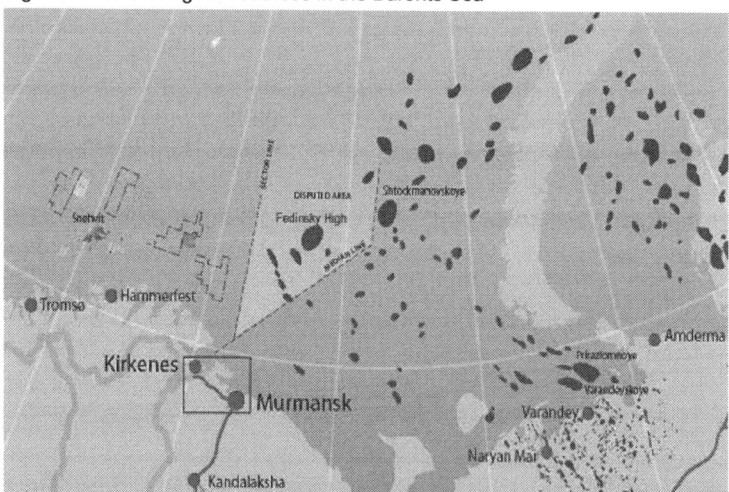

Source: http://www.arcticportal.org/old-news/481-russia-to-explore-barents-sea-shelf

In 1957, Norway and the USSR agreed on their first maritime boundary in the Arctic. This boundary runs from the northern end point of the land boundary in a northeastern direction through the Varangerfjord and terminates on the Varangerfjord's closing line, thereby not extending into the Barents Sea. It was not until after each country claimed exclusive rights to the continental shelf in 1963 and 1968 that Norway and Russia entered into informal talks about their maritime boundary in the Barents Sea in 1970. Oslo and Moscow agreed to conduct negotiations on the basis of Article 6 of the multilateral Convention on the Continental Shelf of 1958 (United Nations 1958). However, Norway's and Russia's different perceptions of delimitation of the maritime territory in the Barents Sea brought negotiations to a halt.

Moscow has traditionally based its position on a sector line, running roughly along longitude 32 E northwards from the Russian coastline. Oslo, on the contrary, has based its position on an equidistance (median) line between the coasts on either side of the border. It was the continental shelf between these two lines, of approximately 155000 km² (and the overlapping EEZs within this area) that constituted the disputed area in the Barents Sea. In addition to this, there were overlapping claims further north in the Arctic Ocean, of approximately 20000 km². Altogether the disputed area was approximately 175000 km².

In 1977, the talks between Oslo and Moscow became further complicated by the establishment of a 200 nm (nautical mile) Norwegian EEZ and a 200 nm Soviet Fishery Zone. These zones were not completely identical with the countries' continental shelf claims in the region. The so-called "Loop Hole" in the middle of the Barents Sea constituted an area of some 62400 km² of high seas that was completely surrounded by the Norwegian and Russian 200 nm zones. Both Oslo and Moscow agreed to draw a single maritime boundary for the continental shelf and the EEZ, but they still were unable to agree on the boundary line.

However, Oslo and Moscow realized the necessity of regulating foreign fishing activities in the Barents Sea and, for this reason, signed a provisional fishing agreement in 1978 (the so-called

"Grey Zone Agreement"). This agreement was initially designed for one year, but it remains in force, having been renewed annually. Its geographical scope is different from the previously disputed area. It applies to a total area of 67500 km², of which 23000 km² were in undisputed Norwegian waters and 3000 km² were in undisputed Russian waters.

There were ups and downs in the Norwegian-Soviet/Russian negotiations over the following years. For example, in 1991 there were official announcements that the talks were to be finalized soon, but no early agreement was achieved. Through the 1990s and 2000s, regular conflicts between Oslo and Moscow took place because Norway, for ecological reasons, has introduced strict rules and fixed quotas to regulate the fishery in the region which were never been accepted by the Russian side. This led to numerous tensions over the inspection and boarding of Russian fishing boats by the Norwegian Coastal Guards.

Several factors have eventually caused the Norwegian-Russian compromise.

First, Norway and Russia signed and ratified the 1982 United Nations Convention on the Law of the Sea (UNCLOS) (United Nations 1982) in 1996 and 1997, respectively. By doing this they modified the rules applicable to the delimitation of the continental shelf and the EEZ because the UNCLOS provides identical rules for these legal procedures, thus favoring the median rather than sectoral principle of demarcation of maritime territories.

Second, in the 1990s and 2000s the International Court of Justice (ICJ) in The Hague and specially appointed arbitration tribunals have issued decisions that clarified important principles and provided guidance for coastal states. Particularly, the ICJ has specified that the solution is to be based on objective geographical features where any major disparities in the respective coastal lengths may be of significance. Both Norway and Russia took a notice of the ICJ's decisions to solve their dispute in the Barents Sea.

Third, in addition to the above legal factors, both Oslo and Moscow had some serious political reasons to finally strike a deal.

For Norway, such a compromise was important because the dispute with Russia was one of the last ones of that sort in its relations with the Arctic neighbors. In 2006 an agreement between Norway, Iceland, Denmark, and the Faroe Islands on a *modus vivendi* on the delimitation of their common continental shelf beyond 200 nm in the Northeast Atlantic was signed. In 2009 Oslo got a decision from the UNCLCS that formally defined the limits of the Norwegian shelf and EEZ in the Arctic (beyond the Barents Sea). The proposed accord with Moscow would leave the maritime boundary between the outer continental shelves of the Norwegian Svalbard Archipelago and Greenland as the last unresolved boundary issue affecting Norway in the Arctic. The legal experts believe that this issue will likely be resolved soon.

On the other hand, by solving the Barents Sea dispute Moscow could have free hands for continuation of its 'fight' for the underwater Lomonosov and Mendeleev ridges that are potentially rich in hydrocarbons and where its ambitions collide with the Danish and Canadian ones. Moreover, by striking a compromise the two countries could get great PR benefits because now they could present themselves as responsible international actors who were able to solve one of the most complicated international disputes by peaceful methods.

Fourth, the economic interests drove the Norwegian-Russian compromise. Oslo was particularly interested in the development of hydrocarbon deposits in the disputed area because since 2001, oil production on the Norwegian shelf has declined. With the end of the 1980s moratorium on hydrocarbon exploitation and exploration activities in the disputed area, a resumption of those activities and new discoveries could be expected. In case of Russia the need for new hydrocarbon deposits was not that strong as in case of Norway because Moscow had enough fields to develop in the undisputed areas. However, in terms of strategic control over the region which is potentially rich in oil and gas Moscow was interested in reaching an agreement with Oslo to legitimize its territorial ambitions.

Finally, the two sides were psychologically tired of 40-year-long negotiations and were eager for putting an end to the dispute, on the one hand, and having a success story in their bilateral relations, on another.

The 2010 Agreement. In 2007, Oslo and Moscow signed a new document that revised the 1957 agreement by extending the maritime boundary in the Varangerfjord area northwards to the intersection of Norway's preferred median line and Russia's preference, the sector line in the Barents Sea. Norwegian Foreign Minister Jonas Gahr Støre then stated that this agreement should pave a way for an accord on the area of overlapping claims in the Barents Sea.

However, it was not until April 2010 that Norwegian Prime Minister Jens Stoltenberg and Russian President Dmitry Medvedev publicly announced that negotiations had been completed, with the exception of some technicalities. The final agreement was signed in Murmansk, Russia, on September 15, 2010, and has been subsequently approved by the two countries' national parliaments. The document came into force in July 2011.

Oslo has withdrawn some of its territorial claims and Moscow has consented to a shift of the 1926 demarcation line to share the 175,000 km$_2$ of disputed area in two almost equal parts defined by eight points (see figure 9). The northern terminal point of the delimitation line is defined as the intersection of the line drawn through points 7 and 8 and the line connecting the easternmost point and the westernmost point of the still undefined outer limits of the countries' continental shelves (Treaty between the Kingdom of Norway and the Russian Federation 2010).

The agreement allows Russia to exercise such sovereign rights and jurisdiction derived from EEZ jurisdiction that Norway could otherwise exercise in an area east of the maritime delimitation line that lies within 200 nm of the Norwegian mainland and beyond 200 nm off the Russian coast.

Being entered into force, the new agreement terminated the Grey Zone Agreement of 1978. However, this treaty did not alter or adversely affect the Norwegian-Russian cooperation in the field of fisheries. This cooperation was continued, for example, in the Norwegian-Russian Joint Fisheries Commission. The 2010 agreement put an end to the 1980s moratorium on the exploration and exploitation of hydrocarbon resources. However, the treaty did not provoke unhealthy competition in this field. Rather, it has some provisions for the coordinated exploitation of transboundary hydrocarbon resources.

Implications of the 2010 Norwegian-Russian Agreement. In Norway, the Agreement has been ratified unanimously and is considered very positively, while in Russia strong debates on the documents' negative consequences ended up by the ratification by the State Duma only because of the constitutional majority of the ruling United Russia party. Both political and expert communities are split up in two almost equal parts, as well as the disputed area.

The main arguments of the Treaty's opponents boil down to the following: first, the Treaty is an "unjustified concession" of the sovereign area to Norway, and, second, the content of the Treaty is not sufficiently elaborated with regard to its future application (Baliev 2011; Reut 2011).

Figure 9. Delimitation of maritime territories in the Barents Sea in accordance with the 2010 Norwegian-Russian treaty

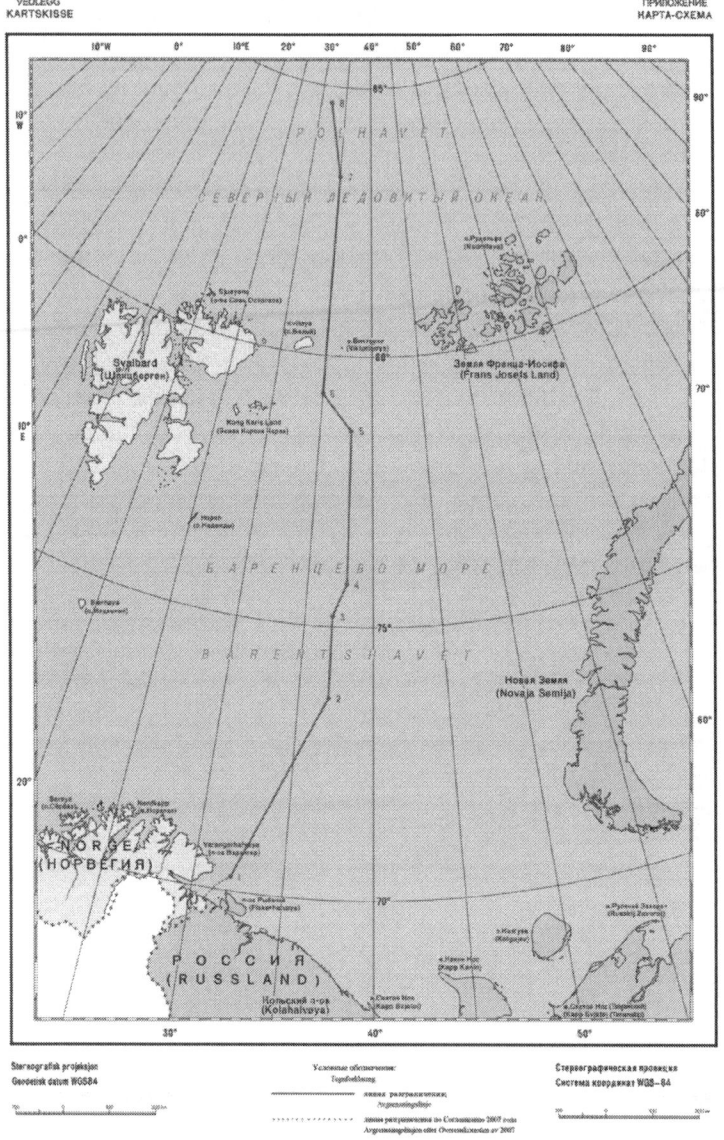

Source: https://commons.wikimedia.org/wiki/File:Map_borderline_at_sea_Norway_Russia.gif. Public domain.

The first argument is rather emotional, although having its own rationale in claiming that the Russian-Norwegian relations are far from being ideal in practice. There are contradictions over fisheries and continuing discussions over the "administrative sovereignty" of Norway at Svalbard/Spitsbergen. Thus, the only reason to sign the Treaty is the possibilities of hydrocarbons extraction, which actually would be possible only in a long-term perspective.

The second argument, although being strictly judicial, partly overlaps with the first counter-Treaty argument named above. It is stated that the Treaty disregards such an important issue as the regime of sea and shelf areas adjacent to Svalbard, which might have negative effect on the work of Russian companies in the region. On the other hand, the proponents of the Treaty maintain that by signing the agreement both Norway and Russia clarified their maritime boundary in the Barents Sea, thereby ensuring predictability and legal certainty in the region. This is important for enacting and enforcing by the two countries environmental rules and fishery regulations as well as for the future exploration and exploitation of hydrocarbon resources in the area.

By concluding the 2010 agreement, Oslo and Moscow demonstrated their eagerness to settle remaining disputes that create obstacles to the international economic cooperation in the region. Particularly, the 2010 agreement can facilitate a future settlement of the residual dispute on the interpretation of the Paris Treaty on Svalbard of 1920 (see next section).

The 2010 agreement has also demonstrated that in resolving their territorial disputes Norway and Russia are committed to the international law, particularly to the UNCLOS and, in a broader context, to the principles of the Ilulissat Declaration of 2008 that confirmed the eagerness of the five Arctic coastal states (A-5) to solve disputes between them by peaceful means, on the basis of international law (Ilulissat Declaration 2008). Finally, Oslo and Moscow signaled to other A-5 states that by adopting a common policy on conflict resolution they can reinforce their claim to leadership on Arctic affairs against emerging actors such as the EU and East Asian countries.

Problems Pertaining to Svalbard

The Svalbard archipelago is located halfway between mainland Norway and the North Pole. It is surrounded by the Norwegian Sea and the Greenland Sea to the west, the Barents Sea to the east and the Arctic Ocean to the north. The land territories of the archipelago cover approximately 62 700 km², whereof about 54 per cent are ice-covered. The largest island of the archipelago is called Spitsbergen, until 1925 this name was used to refer to the whole archipelago. The administrative centre of Longyearbyen and the other inhabited areas of the archipelago are located on this island.

The status of Svalbard is regulated by the Paris Treaty concerning the archipelago of Spitsbergen of 9 February 1920 that recognized full Norwegian sovereignty over the archipelago and required Norway to ensure certain rights for other contracting parties' nationals (Treaty Concerning the Archipelago of Spitsbergen 1920). The USSR formally recognized Norwegian sovereignty over the archipelago in 1924, in an exchange of notes with Norway. The Soviet Union became a party to the Treaty in 1935. Today, there are about 40 States Parties to the Treaty.

Although Russia and Norway have solved their 40-year dispute on the delimitation of maritime territories in the Barents Sea the two countries still have several unresolved questions concerning the Svalbard Archipelago.

The first problem stems from Oslo's decision to establish the Fisheries Protection Zone which is a 200-nautical-mile zone of fisheries jurisdiction zone around the Svalbard archipelago (see figure 10). It was established on 3 June 1977 pursuant to the Act of 17 December 1976 relating to the EEZ of Norway. It should be noted that Norway chose in 1977 until further notice to establish a 200-mile fisheries protection zone rather than a full EEZ. According to Oslo's official position, the main purpose of the zone was to ensure the protection and sound management of the living resources, since this is one of the most important nursery areas for important fish stocks. Norway underlines that as a coastal State, it has a special responsibility for the management of the living resources in these areas. The Norwegian legal experts maintain that rules governing the zone are formulated in such a way that they would not be in conflict with those of the 1920 Treaty. They also believe that these regulatory measures take into account previous foreign fishing patterns in the area and that even though Oslo has a legal right to reserve fishing in the zone exclusively for Norwegian fishermen, its management practices are non-discriminatory (Fife 2013).

Russia (similar to some other signatories to the Paris Treaty) does not recognize the aforementioned decision by Norway and considers this area open to international economic activities, including fishing (Portsel' 2011). Norway regarded such fishing as poaching and a number of arrests of Russian trawlers by the Norwegian coastal guards took place over the last two decades. In 2004 Russia's Northern Fleet started regular patrols of the waters around Svalbard to protect Russian trawlers. The Norwegian side interpreted such practice as illegal, viewing it as a sign of Russian imperialistic ambitions and of Moscow's unwillingness to cooperate with Oslo to settle economic disputes. The 2010 Russian-Norwegian Treaty did not solve the problem and the freedom of the Russian fishing around Svalbard remains an open question.

Figure 10. Norwegian maritime boundaries

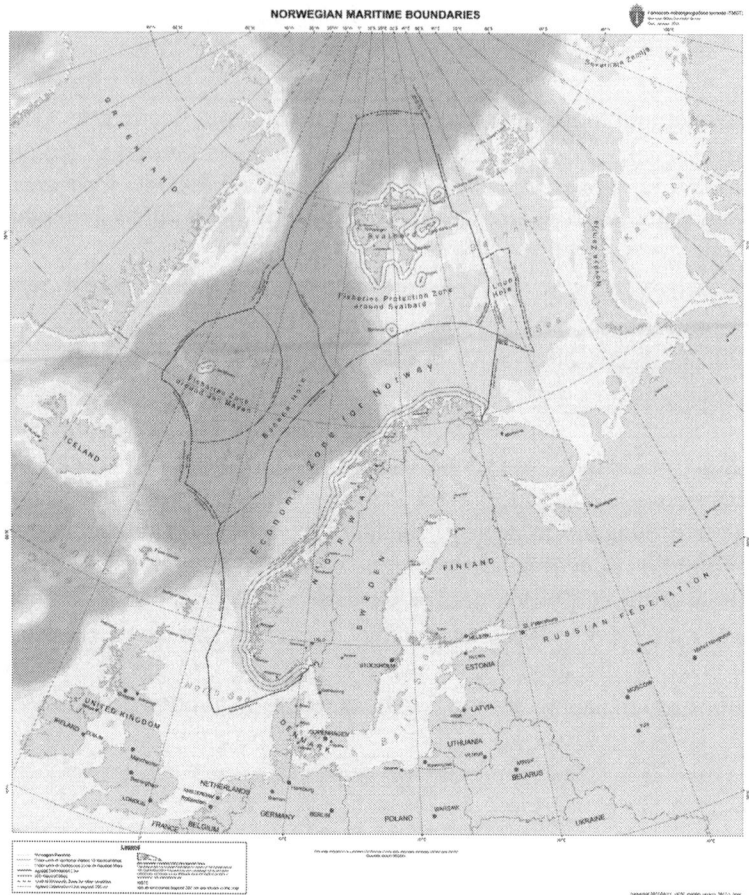

Source: http://www.regjeringen.no/en/dep/ud/selected-topics/civil--rights/Spesi ellfolkerett/folkerettslige-sporsmal-i-tilknytning-ti.html?id=537481 (Map printed with the permission of FMGT, and illegal reproduction is prohibited)

Another problem is related to Russia's potential economic activities on the archipelago's shelf and concerns the significant difference in taxation levels between mainland Norway and the archipelago (Portsel' 2011). Russian companies accessing the Svalbard continental shelf believe that they should enjoy the rights which are envisaged in the 1920 Paris Treaty, particularly the right to pay taxes less than 1 percent of the cost of the hydrocarbons produced. But as Russian international law specialist Alexander Oreshenkov explained, "If a deposit beginning within the limits of the archipelago's territory extends beyond its territorial waters, the Russian companies will be expected to observe the norms of Norway's continental mainland petroleum legislation, which means that 78 percent of their earnings from the hydrocarbons produced outside Norway's territorial waters will go away in tax payments to the Norwegian treasury" (Oreshenkov 2010). These financial stakes are bound to be at the core of future negotiations.

The Russian presence on Svalbard remains the subject of conflict as well. For example, the plans to build a fish-processing plant, which will compete with Norwegian firms, were not well received. In recent years, the Norwegian governor of Spitsbergen has taken a whole series of restrictive measures: he has expanded nature conservation zones to which access by Russian scientists and tourists is restricted or prohibited, required helicopters to obtain advance permission before landing, and introduced rules for the registration of all scientific projects in a special data base. When the Russian side responded to these measures by denying Norwegian scientists investigating biological resources in the Barents Sea access to the Russian EEZ, this was viewed as a discriminatory act.

Despite these disputes both Moscow and Oslo believe that problems pertaining to Svalbard can be solved in the foreseeable future through negotiations and on the basis of international law.

Russian Claims on the Arctic Continental Shelf

According to the UNCLOS, a coastal state has exclusive sovereign rights to explore and exploit the natural resources of its continental shelf up to 200 nautical miles from its shores. Beyond this limit, a coastal state has to provide scientific evidence to establish the extent of the legally defined continental shelf up to 150 nautical miles to exercise the same rights. According to international law, a coastal state can exploit living and non-living resources of the shelf's seabed and subsoil, but these rights do not extend to resources in the water column such as fish stocks, which are covered by a separate regime. The application should be submitted to the UN CLCS, a review body of scientists created under UNCLOS. The CLCS covers continental-shelf claims beyond the 200 nautical miles zone, up to a maximum of 350 nautical miles. It should be noted that the CLCS's ruling is final and binding one.

Due to marine research that has been systematically made in the High North since the Soviet time, in 2001 Russia became the first country to apply to the UNCLCS.

Other coastal states (except the U.S. which did not ratify the UNCLOS) followed Russia. For example, Norway was the second (after Russia) to submit its application to the CLCS in 2006 and the first one among the Arctic state to get a positive decision from the Commission.

In its 2001 claim, Russia argued that the Lomonosov Ridge and the Alpha-Mendeleev Ridge are both geological extensions of its continental Siberian shelf and, thus, that parts of the Central Arctic Ocean, as well as parts of the Barents Sea, the Bering Sea, and the Sea of Okhotsk, fall under its jurisdiction. In effect Russia claimed sovereign rights over resources on the seabed area of some 1.2 million km^2 outside the 200-mile line (see http://www.un.org/Depts/los/clcs_new/submissions_files/rus01/RUS_CLCS_01_2001_LOS_2.jpg).

However, the CLCS found the substantiation of the Russian claim on the shelf insufficient and asked for more information. To collect data and make a new submission comprehensive research expeditions have been organized. The expedition of 2007 with flag planting as a by-product was one of them.

Interestingly, in preparing a new submission Russia used not only the academia but also the military. For example, the objective of the Russian Navy's mission within the framework of the expedition *Arktika-2012* was to prove that its landmass extends to the North Pole by drilling into the sea floor to collect rock samples for scientific analysis. In September 2012, the *Kalitka*, a *Losharik*-

class nuclear-powered auxiliary submarine, was used to guide the *Kapitan Dranitsyn* and *Dickson* ice breakers in drilling three boreholes at two different sites on the Mendeleev ridge, collecting over 500 kg of rock samples (International Institute for Strategic Studies 2012).

In August 2015, Russia has officially resubmitted its application for the extension of its Arctic shelf (http://www.un.org/depts/los/clcs_new/submissions_files/rus01_rev15/2015_08_03_Exec_Summary_English.pdf). The CLCS plans to start its reviewing in 2016.

International experts suggest several scenarios for the further developments if a second, revised submission be returned by the CLCS. One extreme would be for Moscow to withdraw from the UNCLOS and just declare unilaterally that its continental shelf reaches up to the North Pole. Russia would still retain the right to a continental shelf, and would find itself in the same position as the U.S., which remains outside the UNCLOS, and would have to rely on customary law to support its claim. However, this option is hardly acceptable for Moscow because it would provide a much less secure legal position than would a CLCS' decision which is considered as a final and binding ruling.

The strong nationalistic groupings in Russia would support such unilateralism. However, Russia's official policy undoubtedly lies within the UNCLOS framework. Russia has much to lose if it undermines the authority of the UNCLOS in the Arctic. Moscow tries to avoid a conflict situation because any conflict, even if not armed, would prove to the world that the UNCLOS does not work and weaken the legitimacy of the Convention. Such weakening is seen by Moscow as dangerous and unacceptable.

As Moe (2014) put it, the other extreme scenario would be to accept that the initial submission was too ambitious and not substantiated by geophysical research and come back to the Commission with a revised, less expansive position. On the one hand, this alternative would definitely show respect for international law. However, on the other hand, such an initiative would entail large domestic political costs for a Russian leader who would dare to abandon Russia's ambitious Arctic claim.

Both foreign and Russian experts do not exclude one more, third, scenario which, they believe, is both possible and the most likely. That option is Moscow's agreement to postpone the revision the new submission by the CLCS (Moe 2014; Zagorsky 2013). First, it will take the CLCS years or even decades to consider the existing and forthcoming applications. Even if it becomes clear that the Russian claims on the Lomonosov and Mendeleev ridges cannot be substantiated, all the Arctic states may decide that it is better to agree on disagreement and continue business as usual. Besides the need to preserve the UNCLOS in the Arctic, also a realistic assessment of their economic interests and technical capabilities prevent them from a conflict over the disputed areas. These areas are very deep and extraction of oil and gas there will not become profitable for many decades.

Moreover, as the most authoritative assessment of Arctic mineral resources from the US Geological Survey maintains, most hydrocarbon resources are likely to be found in relatively shallower waters, within the 200-mile limit (U.S. Geological Survey 2008). Most of these uncontroversial continental shelves are relatively unexplored and the conflicting parties first should develop them.

In any case, as Moscow repeatedly underlined, the Kremlin plans to solve the problem within the UNCLOS framework, peacefully and on the basis of a solid research data.

Chapter 9.
Russian Military Strategies in the Arctic.

The Russian military strategy in the High North is a subject of particular criticism from the Western politicians and experts. They believe that the Russian force modernization programs and military activities violate the existing regional military balance and provoke a new round of arms race in the Arctic (Borgerson, 2009; Huebert, 2010; Huebert et al., 2012; Smith and Giles, 2007; Zysk, 2008). Russia's critics suggest that the Ukrainian crisis has demonstrated Moscow's willingness to use military-coercive instruments to protect its national interests, including those in the Arctic. Moscow denies these allegations and points out that it can use military power only as a last resort to defend itself in case of foreign aggression or attack on its critical objects in the region.

It is an ambition of this chapter to discuss the question whether Russia is really a military revisionist power in the Arctic or it can be evaluated in different, more positive, terms, particularly as a country that is interested in the region's stability and open to international cooperation in this part of the world? However, before addressing this main research question the Russian threat perceptions should be analyzed.

Threat perceptions

Since the general focus of the Arctic policies had shifted from hard to soft security (see the Introduction) the Russian threat perceptions have also evolved significantly over the last two decades. Moscow is no longer concerned about the threat of a large-scale nuclear war and pays now the greater attention to threats and challenges that stem from the climate change and growing competition over the Arctic natural resources and sea routes rather than from the military sphere. Now the Russian national security structures are charged not only with purely military functions but also with things like cleaning the Soviet-made environmental mess,

SAR operations, fighting oil spills, poaching, smuggling and illegal migration.

It should be noted that some climate change implications such as, for example, the Northern pole ice cap's meltdown necessitate some serious changes in the Arctic states' military strategies, including the Russian one. On the one hand, as the recent U.S. Navy's document argues, the extension of the ice-free season can result in a significant expansion of surface naval activities in the Arctic (The United States Navy Arctic Roadmap for 2014 to 2030, 2014: 8, 16–19). However, on the other hand, the shrinking ice cap provides less protection to submarines making them visible for enemy's satellites and aircraft.

Along with the significant economic and environmental interests the Russian perceptions of the Arctic to a larger extent are still based on hard security considerations. For example, the Kola Peninsula and the adjacent area are still considered a region of special strategic importance to Russia's national security. The direct access to the Arctic and Atlantic oceans, a relatively close proximity to potential U.S./NATO targets, and a relatively developed military infrastructure make this region well-suited for strategic naval operations (Khramchikhin 2011 and 2013). The strategic importance of the Kola Peninsula is above all explained by the fact that it hosts two-thirds of the Russian sea-based nuclear forces. As some military analysts emphasize, the nuclear deterrent remains not only a key element of the Russian military strategy, but serves also as a symbol and guarantee of Russia's great power status (Zysk, 2008: 81). Maintaining strategic nuclear capabilities is, therefore, one of the highest priorities of Russia's military policies both in the High North and globally.

The Russian military analysts believe that the Archangelsk Air Defense Sector is still crucial for the prevention of surprise attack over the North Pole. The Norwegian Sea still can serve as the main launch area for Western seaborne attack, so, these analysts maintain, the Russian Navy should still be concerned about the readiness of its anti-submarine forces in the Arctic (Khramchikhin 2011 and 2013).

Both the Russian politicians and military repeatedly point to allegedly increasing political and military pressures from the U.S. and other NATO member states in the North. They believe that the West/NATO want to undermine Russia's positions in the region. They emphasize the fact that Russian armed forces in the High North are still facing NATO just across the border. The Arctic coastal states' armed forces modernization programs are predominantly treated in the alarmist way.

While the American experts believe that Washington has quite modest military-strategic ambitions in the Arctic (Corgan 2014), Moscow is worried about the recent U.S. military strategy in the Arctic that envisages Washington's increased security activities in the region. Moscow was especially concerned about the U.S. plans to increase its readiness to conduct maritime and air patrol and interception operations; to exercise and assert its navigation and overflight rights and freedoms in the region; to ensure its access to global commons in the Arctic; to expand its power projection capabilities, etc. (U.S. Department of Defense, 2013; The United States Navy Arctic Roadmap for 2014 to 2030, 2014).

Given the ice-free Arctic in the foreseeable future (at least for the part of the year) the Russian military analysts do not exclude the possibility that the U.S. could permanently deploy a nuclear submarine fleet and sea-based ABM systems in the Arctic Ocean (Khramchikhin, 2013; Russia fears missile defense, 2009). In this case the U.S. will create capabilities for intercepting Russian ballistic missile launches and making a preventive strike. For the above reasons, this school of strategic thought recommends Russia not only to keep its strategic forces at the present level but also to regularly modernize them.

President Vladimir Putin has immediately reacted to the new U.S. doctrine by ordering the Russian Defense Ministry to accelerate the creation of the AGF, modernization of the Northern Fleet and reopening the Soviet-time air and naval bases along the NSR (President Putin, 2013).

It should be noted that there is some difference in threat perceptions between the Russian strategic and operative-tactical forces. For the Russian strategic forces, the Arctic, North Atlantic and North Pacific create a single operation zone or military theatre where they confront the U.S. strategic forces. For the conventional forces, the Arctic is an area where they should mainly protect Russia's economic interests and state borders (land, maritime and air). From the operative-tactical point of view, the Arctic is split to several sectors which represent various zones of responsibility. In the Western sector, the Russian land and air forces confront the NATO (Norwegian) troops while the conventional component of the Northern Fleet protects Russia's economic interests in the Barents Sea and provides nuclear forces with auxiliary services. The Northern Fleet and Border Guards are responsible for the protection of the NSR and the Arctic Ocean's coastline while the Pacific Fleet controls the Bering Sea, Bering Strait and the access to the Chukchi Sea.

To sum up Russia's threat perceptions, there is a clear tendency towards the increasing role of the soft security-related interests such as ensuring Russia's access to the natural resources and transport routes in the region, climate change mitigation and cleaning up the environmental mess. At the same time, as some Russian strategists believe, there are a number of security threats and challenges in the region that require preservation and further development of a certain military potential and presence in the North. They took a notice that the ongoing Ukrainian crisis has negatively affected the overall Russia's relations with NATO and its member states which unilaterally suspended several cooperative projects with Russia, including military-to-military contacts and the development of confidence and security-building measures.

Military activities and modernization plans

Contrary to the Western alarmists' worries about Moscow's military pre-eminence in the North the Russian military presence in the region has considerably decreased over the last two decades. Both components—naval and air force—of the Russian armed forces in the region are inferior to the NATO ones (see tables 2 and 3).

It should be also noted that in contrast with the Cold War period when Russian military strategies in the North were dictated by the logic of global political and military confrontation between two superpowers (USSR and USA) or two military blocs (Warsaw Pact and NATO), the current Moscow' military policies in the region are driven by completely different motives. As the threat of a global nuclear war has disappeared, these strategies aim at three major goals: first, to demonstrate and ascertain Russia's sovereignty over the AZRF (including the EEZ and continental shelf); second, to protect its economic interests in the North; and third, to demonstrate that Russia retains its great power status and has world-class military capabilities.

Table 2. The Russian armed forces in the North

	USSR in 1980s	Russia in 2010s
Submarines	172	30
-of them SSBN	39	7
SSBN in permanent patrol	10–12 (6–7 in Arctic)	1–2
Aircraft carriers	2	1
Larger ships	74	17
Auxiliary vessels	200	33
Aircrafts	400	100
Helicopters	-	40

Source: Arbatov, 2011.

Table 3. U.S. and NATO forces capable to operate in the North

	U.S. in 1980s	U.S. in 2010s	NATO in 2010s
Submarines	78	33	85
-of them SSBN	28	6	8
SSBN in permanent patrol	-	6–8	-
Submarines armed with cruise missiles Tomahawk	-	39	-
Aircraft carriers	7	4	6
Larger ships	90	49	100
Amphibious assault ships	24	14	-
Aircraft	700	360	200

Source: Arbatov, 2011.

The demonstration of Russia' military power and its regional presence in the Arctic are mainly done through strategic bomber and naval patrols as well as land and naval exercises.

The air force is perceived by Moscow as a central element in its demonstration of power. Over-flights of Russian military aircraft over the Arctic fell from 500 per year during the Soviet period, to only half a dozen in the 1990s and at the start of the 2000s. In 2007, Russian strategic bombers flew over the Arctic for the first time since the end of the Cold War. Two Tu-95MS, based in the Saratov region at the Engels aviation base with mid-flight refueling capability, now regularly patrol the region. These over-flights drew heavy criticism from Norway, Canada, UK and the U.S. which have seen these patrols as evidence of Russia's return to the Soviet-like military practices and growing strategic ambitions in the North. However, as most authoritative Western military experts point it out, the resumption of the strategic bomber patrols may be interpreted more in terms of the desire not to lose capacities and, above all, as a political tool rather than the sign of a renewed aggressiveness in the region (Lasserre et al., 2012: 16; Laruelle, 2014: 128–129).

As far as the air force potential available for operations in the North is concerned, Russia's air assets consist mainly of the aircraft supporting the Northern Fleet or stationed in northern Russia. Many of these do not have the range for operations in the Arctic area outside Russia (Wezeman, 2012: 9). In addition, Russia has a fleet of ageing long- and medium-range bombers most which are located outside the AZRF. There are 63 turbo-propelled Tu-95MSs which are very old (designed in the 1950s) but still the mainstays of the Russian strategic aviation. The Russian air force also has 18 more modern, long-range Tu-160 *Blackjacks* bombers, as well as 80 Tu-22M *Backfire* medium bombers that were especially feared by NATO in the Cold War period for their anti-ship capacities. It should be noted that these planes are not stealthy and are easily detected when flying at high altitude, despite additional electronic countermeasures recently added to the Tu-160 and Tu-22M. Moreover, the shortage of mid-air refueling tankers remains the most serious problem affecting the operational capabilities of Russian strategic aviation. The airfield *Temp* on the Kotelny Island (Novosibirsky Archipelago) although with quite limited and dual-use (military and civilian) capacities has been reactivated in 2013 (Zagorsky, 2013). Several other Arctic air bases in Alykel', Amderma, Anadyr', Nagurskoe, Naryan-Mar, Rogachevo and Tiksi are to be reactivated in the foreseeable future (Shoigu sozdast, 2013).

No credible plans to modernize the above fleet are known. In 2009, the Russian government granted a contract to Tupolev company to develop a new stealth bomber the PAK-DA that would replace the Tu-22M, the Tu-160 and the Tu-95MS. The prototype is scheduled to fly in 2020 and the aircraft is expected to enter service only in 2025–30. However, these plans can be changed if other programs (for example, the 5th generation fighter Sukhoi T-50/PAK-FA) would become a more important priority for the Russian Air Force. Because of the long time frame for the development of the PAK-DA, it was decided to upgrade the Tu-22M and produce 10 more Tu-160s before 2020. Some experts suggest that probably many present Russian strategic and medium-range bombers will no longer be operational by 2025–2030 and the air force will then be left only with its ageing Tu-160 and Tu-95 fleet (Lasserre et al., 2012: 17–18).

As far as the naval patrolling is concerned, since 2007 Russia resumed long-range patrols in different parts of the world. This was symbolized by the patrols undertaken by the nuclear-powered guided-missile cruiser *Peter the Great* through the Mediterranean and Caribbean Seas, Atlantic, Indian and Pacific oceans (2008–2010). In 2008, Russia confirmed that it was expanding its current level of operations in the Arctic. The Navy resumed its warship presence in the Arctic ocean with military ships patrolling near Norwegian and Danish defense zones. It also increased the operational radius of the Northern Fleet's submarines, and under-ice training for submariners has become a priority task.

Russia has ambitious plans to modernize its navy deployed to the High North. For example, after the *Peter the Great*'s successful trip around the world in 2008–2009, the Ministry of Defense announced that it would upgrade three other heavy nuclear-powered missile cruisers, the *Admiral Lazarev*, the *Admiral Nakhimov*, and the *Admiral Ushakov*. Currently, the *Admiral Kuznetsov*, the only Russia aircraft carrier, operates with the Northern Fleet, hosting twenty fighters and ten anti-submarine helicopters on board. The destroyer *Vice-Admiral Kulakov*, recently repaired, was integrated into the Northern Fleet in 2011. The naval aviation includes 200 combat aircraft and fifty helicopters.

Looking at the problems that the Northern Fleet currently faces, it should be noted that the fleet needs coastal ships and frigates able to conduct rapid intervention operations. Several are currently under construction, but they have already experiences numerous delays. The project to build eight *Admiral Gorshkov* class and six *Krivak* class frigates which is constantly delayed will not be enough to renew Russia's ocean-going surface ships. There were plans to purchase two or four *Mistrals* helicopter carriers from France. However, it was decided to limit these plans to building only two vessels and deploy them to the Pacific fleet, not the Northern one.

Keeping nuclear deterrence capabilities is crucial for the future of the Northern Fleet. The older sea-based nuclear deterrent is in the process of deep modernization. Presently, Russia has six operational Delta III and six Delta IV strategic submarines. According to the Russian Defense Ministry, there are no plans to modernize the older Delta III class submarines. They were built during the 1980s and will be decommissioned in the near future. Only the Delta IV submarines undergo the process of modernization. They will be provided with a new sonar system and the new intercontinental ballistic missile (ICBM) *Sineva* (Skiff SSN-23) which entered service in 2007. *Sineva* is a third-generation liquid-propelled ICBM which is able to cover a distance up to 8,300 km and to carry either four or ten nuclear warheads (http://www.arms-expo.ru/049055051051124052049049.html). Russia is planning to equip its Delta IV class submarines with at least 100 *Sineva* missiles which are to stay on alert status until 2030. The *Sineva* missiles can be launched from under the ice while remaining invisible to enemy's satellites until the last moment (Laruelle, 2014: 122).

Another class of the Russian strategic submarines, the *Typhoons* which are considered as the world's largest, will be re-equipped with long-range cruise missiles. For the time-being, only one *Typhoon*-class strategic submarine, the *Dmitri Donskoy*, has been modernized and deployed to the Northern Fleet. It serves to conduct test firing for the *Bulava* system, a new generation solid-fuel SLBM, designed to avoid possible future U.S. anti-ballistic missile defense weapons, and which can cover a distance of more than 9,000 kilometers (http://www.arms-expo.ru/049057054048124050052056054051.html).

It is planned that in the future, the *Typhoon*-class submarines should be replaced with the new *Borey*-class fourth generation nuclear-powered strategic submarines. The first *Borey*-class submarine, the *Yuri Dolgoruky*—that was the first strategic submarine to be built in Russia since the collapse of the Soviet Union—has been in operation by the Northern Fleet since January 2013. Two other *Borey*-class submarines, the *Alexander Nevsky* and the *Vladimir Monomakh*, run the sea trials and the fourth one, *Prince Vladimir*, is under construction at the Severodvinsk shipyard (http://bastion-karpenko.narod.ru/955_more_01.html). These three submarines will be placed with the Pacific Fleet. The *Borey*-class submarines which are to be deployed to the Northern Fleet will be based at the Gadzhievo navy base (about 100 kilometers from the Norwegian border), where new infrastructure is being built to host them. This new generation of the Russian strategic submarines is almost invisible at deep ocean depths and—having several types of cruise missiles and torpedoes—it will be able to carry out multi-purpose missions, including attacks on enemy aircraft carriers and missile strikes on coastal targets. According to the Defense Ministry's plans, the building of eight *Borey*-class submarines (four for the Northern Fleet and four for the Pacific one) should be completed by 2020, which once again seems too ambitious and unlikely.

To provide the logistical and administrative support to the Northern Fleet a new Arctic Centre for Material and Technical Support with a staff of more than 15,000 was created in 2012.

As far as the land forces are concerned until recently there were two major units—the 200th independent motorized infantry brigade and marine brigade—both based nearby Pechenga (Murmansk region) close to the Norwegian border town of Kirkenes. There were plans to reorganize the motorized infantry brigade to the Arctic special force unit, with soldiers trained in a special program and equipped with modern personal equipment for military operations in the Arctic. The Arctic brigade should be operational by 2015 or 2016 (http://www.discred.ru/news/sukhoputnye_voj ska_arkticheskaja_motostrelkovaja_brigada/2012-02-22-977; Wezeman, 2012: 9). According to the former Defense Minister Anatoly Serdyukov, one more Arctic brigade could be created to be located probably in the Arkhangelsk region. However, the current Defense Minister Sergey Shoigu did not confirm these plans referring only to the need to reorganize the 200th brigade (Shoigu sozdast, 2013). No future plans concerning the marine brigade at Pechenga were announced.

However, the Ukrainian crisis has made adjustments to Russia's military planning. While two Pechenga-based brigades were left in place, the Arctic brigade was surprisingly created ahead of the schedule (in January 2015) and deployed in Alakurtti which is close to the Finnish-Russian border (http://yle.fi/uutiset/tass_ rossiya_nachala_razmeshchenie_voisk_v_alakurtti_vozle_granitsy _s_finlyandiyei/7735585).

Along with the army, air force and navy, the efforts to strengthen the Border Guards Service's (which is subordinated to the FSS) control over the region were made. An Arctic border guards unit was created as early as in 1994. Its aim was to monitor the circulation of ships and poaching at sea. The unit was reorganized in 2004–2005. In 2009, it was announced that new Arctic units had been established in border guard stations in Arkhangelsk and Murmansk. They started to patrol the NSR—for the first time since the Soviet time. Now the border guards assigned with the task to deal with the new—soft security—threats and challenges such as the establishment of reliable border control systems, the introduction of special visa regulations to certain regions, and the implementation of technological controls over fluvial zones and sites along the NSR. It is currently controlled from the air by border guard aircrafts and on the land and sea by the North-Eastern Border Guard Agency; the Russian border guards further plan to establish a global monitoring network from Murmansk to Wrangel Island. All in all, Moscow plans to build 20 border guard stations along the Arctic Ocean's coastline (Zagorsky, 2013).

As mentioned above all the conventional forces in the AZRF should be united under the auspices of the AGF led by the joint Arctic command. Given an 'increased NATO military threat' in the North President Putin has decided to accelerate the creation of a new strategic command 'North' which was done in December 2014 (Gavrilov 2014).

All the power structures (army, navy, border guards and the Ministry of Emergency Situations) are charged with implementing the AC agreement of 2011 on the creation of a Maritime and Aeronautical Sea and Rescue System. Each country is responsible for its sector of the Arctic and Russia has the biggest one. The SAR agreement's signatories undertake joint exercises on the regular basis. As many experts believe, the SAR activities are a clear sign of the shift from the armed forces' purely military functions to the soft security missions.

To sum up, the Russian modernization programs do not affect the regional military balance. The most impressive programs are related to the modernization of the strategic forces that have global rather than regional missions. As far as the conventional/general purpose forces are concerned they will be at the same or reduced level. It should be noted that other Arctic coastal states have also begun to upgrade their military equipment and military doctrines with a view to a better control of the North, but it has nothing to do with an arms race. As, for example, the Canadian Standing Committee on National Defense concluded in its 2010 report, "there is no immediate military threat to Canadian territories. [...] The challenges facing the Arctic are not of the traditional military type. [...] Rather than sovereignty threats we face what might best be termed policing threat. These do not require combat capability" (http://www.parl.gc.ca/HousePublications/Publication.aspx?DocId=4486644&File=21&Language=E&Mode=1&Parl=40&Ses=3).

Conclusions

As Russia's both strategic documents and practical policies demonstrate Moscow has extremely important national interests in the region. These interests include the access to and exploitation of the AZRF natural resources (mineral and biological ones). Russia tries to modernize and further develop the AZRF's industrial base which makes a significant and valuable contribution to the country's economy. Moscow is also interested in opening up of the NSR for international commercial traffic and developing circumpolar air routes. Moscow is deeply concerned about the environmental situation in the AZRF. Russia still has considerable military-strategic interests in the region and tries to modernize its armed forced located there. Similar to other coastal states Moscow sees its military presence in the region as an efficient instrument to demonstrate its sovereignty over and protect its national interests in the High North.

In general terms, Moscow's Arctic policies represent a combination—sometimes quite eclectic—of the hard and soft power approaches. On the one hand, Moscow is quite assertive as regards its claims on the Arctic continental shelf. The Russian military modernization programs in the High North are seen by other Arctic players as excessive and destabilizing the regional strategic balance. The Russian international partners are also concerned about the lack of serious progress in Russia's environmental strategies and its policies toward the indigenous people.

However, on the other hand, it is possible to identify a number of positive changes in Moscow's Arctic policies. Conceptually, the Russian leadership now realizes that most of threats and challenges to the AZRF originate from inside rather than outside of the country. These problems are caused by the complex of factors such as the degradation the Soviet-made economic, transport and social infrastructures in the region, the current resource-oriented model of the Russian economy, the lack of funds and managerial skills to develop the AZRF, etc. For this reason, Russia's current strategy aims at solving existing domestic problems rather than focuses on external expansion.

Moscow understands that the success of its Arctic strategy, to a larger extent, depends on how effective its socio-economic and environmental policies in the region are. The Russian decision-making and academic communities managed to develop an integrated approach to the sustainable development strategy in the AZRF. The stimuli to innovatively develop the AZRF industrial sector were created by the government over the last 10–15 years. At the same time, the serious efforts to balance the industrial development plans with the needs of indigenous peoples and Arctic environment were made. It should be noted, however, that the course toward modernization and innovation charted by the Russian government should move from making declarations to the implementation phase involving specific and realistic projects in the AZRF.

Russia's political leadership seems to understand the need for constructive dialogue and deeper political engagement with Russia's Arctic regions, municipalities, indigenous people and NGOs. Moscow encourages these actors to work with international partners (unless it takes the form of separatism or attempts to challenge federal foreign policy prerogatives). The main problem here is implementation again. In reality, the federal bureaucracy's policies are not always conducive to the initiatives of local and civil society institutions. Moscow is also demonstrating a growing willingness to solve the environmental problems of the AZRF and cooperate with international bodies in this sphere. Hopefully, this will result in a more systemic approach to Russian environmental policies in the region, backed by considerable financial support.

As far as Moscow's military strategies in the region is concerned its overall assessment demonstrates that the Russian ambitions in the North may be high, but they are still far from being realized, and they are not necessarily implying the intentions and proper capabilities to confront other regional players by military means. Russia may be eager to develop powerful armed forces in the North, but its plans to modernize its strategic air force, to recreate a strong navy, to modernize its fleet of strategic submarines, to lay down new icebreakers and replace the old ones, to create an AGF, to establish new FSS border control and SAR units are a difficult task. It is hard to imagine that Russia has the financial and technical capacities as well as managerial skills to meet these objectives in the foreseeable future.

It should be noted that the Russian military modernization programs are rather modest and aim to upgrading the Russian armed forces in the High North rather than providing them with additional offensive capabilities or restoring the Soviet-time huge military potential. Given the financial constraints these programs have recently become less ambitious and more realistic. The Russian military increasingly aims at defending the country's economic interests in the region and control over the huge AZRF territory rather than expanding its 'sphere of influence'.

To conclude, in contrast with the internationally wide-spread stereotype of Russia as a hard/revisionist power in the Arctic, there are serious grounds to believe that in the foreseeable future Moscow will pursue quite pragmatic and responsible policies in the region. On the one hand, such a strategy will aim at protecting Russia's legitimate economic and political interests in the High North. On the other hand, Moscow says that it is open to a mutually beneficial cooperation with foreign partners in areas exploiting the Arctic natural resources, developing sea routes, Arctic research and environmental protection.

Russia clearly demonstrates that it prefers to use soft power (diplomatic, economic and cultural methods) rather than hard power (coercive) instruments, as well as to act *via* international organizations. This brings the Russian behavior (at least regionally) closer to the soft power model albeit there is a long way to go to Russia fully fitting in this frame. It should be noted that to consolidate the soft power "pattern" of Russia's behavior and make it sustainable a proper international environment in the Arctic should be created by common efforts. Other regional players should demonstrate their responsibility and willingness to solve existing and potential problems in a quiet/friendly way and on the basis of international law.

References

1990. Agreement between the United States of America and the Union of Soviet Socialist Republics on the Maritime Boundary. http://www.state.gov/documents/organization/125431.pdf

Ahunov, Viktor. 2000. The speech of Mr Viktor Ahunov, Deputy Director General, Ministry for Atomic Energy. In Nissinen, Marja (ed.). Foreign Ministers' Conference on the Northern Dimension, Helsinki, 11–12 November 1999. A Compilation of Speeches. Helsinki: Unit for the Northern Dimension in the Ministry for Foreign Affairs, pp. 73–74.

Alexandrov, Oleg. 2009. Labyrinths of the Arctic Policy. Russia in Global Affairs 3, http://eng.globalaffairs.ru/number/n_13591.

Antrim, Caitlyn. 2010. The New Maritime Arctic. Geopolitics and the Russian Arctic in the 21st Century. Russia in Global Affairs 3. http://eng.globalaffairs.ru/number/The-New-Maritime-Arctic-15000

Arbatov, Alexei. 2011. Arktika I strategicheskaya stabil'nost [The Arctic and strategic stability]. In Arktika: Zona Mira I Sotrudnichestva [The Arctic: Zone of Peace and Cooperation], ed. Andrei Zagorski. Moscow: Institute of World Economy and International Relations, Russian Academy of Sciences, pp. 65–67.

2008. The Arctic Merits the European Union's Attention—First Step Towards an EU Arctic Policy. http://europa.eu/rapid/pressReleasesAction.do?reference=IP/08/1750&format=HTML&aged=0&language=EN&guiLanguage=en

Baranovsky, Vladimir. 2002. Russia's attitudes towards the EU: political aspects. Helsinki: UPI.

Barents Euro-Arctic Council. 2011. Progress in Exclusion of the Barents Environmental "Hot Spots" http://www.beac.st/Hot_Spots_Information_System/Documents_archive/Press_releases.iw3

The Barents Euro-Arctic Council, *The Barents Cooperation* (2013). Available at: www.barentsinfo.fi/beac/docs/Barents_Cooperation_information_English_October_2013.pdf, accessed January 19, 2014.

2008. Basics of the State Policy of the Russian Federation in the Arctic for the Period until 2020 and for a Further Perspective (Moscow; adopted 18 September 2008, promulgated 30 March 2009, published in Rossiyskaya Gazeta in Russian).

Belov, Pyotr. 2012. Resursno-Demograficheskie Aspecty Rossiyskoi Arkticheskoi Geopolitiki [Resource-Demographic Aspects of Russia's Arctic Geopolitics]. In Geopolitika: Teoriya, Istoriya, Praktika [Geopolitics: Theory, History, Practice]. Moscow: Prostranstvo i Vremya.

Blunden M. 2009.The New Problem of Arctic Stability. Survival 51 (5), pp. 123–132.

Borgerson, Scott. 2008. Arctic Meltdown: the Economic and Security Implications of global Warming. Foreign Affairs 87: 2, pp. 66–69.

2009. Canada's Northern Strategy: Our North, Our Heritage, Our Future. http://www.northernstrategy.gc.ca/cns/cns-eng.asp

Caverhill-Godkewitsch, I. (2011). Facing the Future: Canada's Environmental Security Challenges in the 21st Century. Journal of Military and Strategic Studies 3, pp. 1–11.

The Central Executive Committee of the Soviet Union.1964. "Ob Obyavlenii Territoriei SSSR Zemel' I Ostrovov, Raspolozhennykh v Severnom Ledovitom Okeane, 15 Aprelya 1926 g." [On the Proclamation of Lands and Islands Located in the Arctic Ocean as Territory of the USSR, 15 April 1926]. In: Documenty Vneshnei Politiki SSSR [USSR Foreign Policy Documents].Moscow: Politizdat, p. 228. http://xx-vekistoria.narod.ru/libr/istochnik/vnpol/ostovaSLO.html

Commission of European Communities.2008a. Climate Change and International Security. Paper from the High Representative and the European Commission to the European Council. SI 13/08," 14 March. www.consilium.europa.eu/ueDocs/cms_Data/docs/press-Data/en/reports/99387.pdf

Commission of European Communities. 2008b. The European Union and the Arctic Region. Communication from the Commission to the European Parliament and the Council.COM(2008)763 final. November 20. http://eeas.europa.eu/arctic_region/docs/com_08_763_en.pdf

2009. Concept of Sustainable Development of Indigenous Smallnumbered Peoples of the North, Siberia and the Far East of the Russian Federation, Moscow, 4 February 2009, http://government.ru/gov/results/6580/)

Conley, Heather and Kraut, Jamie. 2010. U.S. Strategic Interests in the Arctic. An Assessment of Current Challenges and New Opportunities for Cooperation. A Report of the CSIS Europe Program. Washington, DC: The Center for Strategic and International Studies. http://csis.org/files/publication/100426_Conley_USStrategicInterests_Web.pdf

Corgan, Michael. 2014. The USA in the Arctic: Superpower or Spectator? Security and Sovereignty in the North Atlantic— Small States, Middle Powers and their Maritime Interests. Edited by Lassi Heininen. Palgrave Pivot, 62–79.

De Coning, Cedric, Mandrup, Thomas and Liselotte Odgaard (eds.). 2014. *The BRICS and Coexistence: An Alternative Vision of World Order.* Abingdon: Routledge Taylor & Francis Group.

2011. Denmark, Greenland and the Faroe Islands: Kingdom of Denmark Strategy for the Arctic 2011–2020. http://um.dk/en/ ~/media/UM/English-site/Documents/Politics-and-diplomacy/ Arktis_Rapport_UK_210x270_Final_Web. ashx

Diatlikovich, V. and Grebtsov, I. 2009. Shelf tsveta khaki [Khaki-colored shelf]. Russkii reporter, April, 2–9, p. 28.

Diev, Andrei. 2009. Arkticheskaya Strategiya Rossii [Russia's Arctic Strategy]. http://flot.com/nowadays/concept/navyrole/arcticstrategy.htm

Dobretsov, N.L. and N.P. Pokhilenko. 2010. Mineral resources and development in the Russian Arctic. Russian Geology and Geophysics 51, pp. 98–111.

Duchacek, Ivo. 1986. *The Territorial Dimension of Politics: Within, Among, and Across Nations.* Boulder and London: Westview Press.

Duchacek, Ivo. 1990. "Perforated Sovereignties: Towards a Typology of New Actors in International Relations" in *Federalism and International Relations: The Role of Subnational Units*, ed. Hans Michelmann and Panayotis Soldatos. Oxford: Claredon Press, 1–33.

Dugin, Alexander. 1991. Misterii Evrazii [The Mysteries of Eurasia]. Moscow: Arktogeia.

Dugin, Alexander. 1993. Giperboreiskaia Teoriia. Opyt Ariosofskogo Issledovaniia [Hyperborean Theory. An Experiment in Ariosophic Investigation]. Moscow: Arktogeia, 1993.

Dugin, Alexander. 2002. Metafizika I Geopolitika Prirodnykh Resursov [Metaphysics and Geopolitics of Natural Resources]. http://www.centrasia.ru/newsA.php?st=1039816440

Dunlap W. 2002. Transit Passage in the Russian Arctic Straits. Durham: International Boundaries Research Unit, University of Durham.

Dushkova, Diana and Evseev, Alexander. 2011. Analiz Techogennogo Vozdeistviyana Geosistemy Evropeiskogo Severa Rossii [Analisys of Technogenic Impact on Geosystems of the European Russian North]. Arktika i Sever 4, 1–34. http://narfu.ru/upload/iblock/673/16.pdf

2012. Ekologicheskoe Sostoyanie Impactnykh Raionov Sushi Arkticheskoi Zony Rossiyskoi Federatsii [The Environmental Situation in the Impact Zones of the Terrestrial Parts of the Arctic Zone of the Russian Federation]. http://www.arcticonline.ru/ekologiya/ekologicheskoe-sostoyanie-impaktnyhrajo nov-sushi-arkticheskoj-zony-rossijskoj-federacii

European Commission and EU High Representative 2012. Developing a European Union Policy towards the Arctic Region: Report on progress since 2008 and next steps", Joint Communication of 26 June 2012.

2012. The Federal Law of July 28, 2012, N 132-FZ "On Amendments to Certain Legislative Acts of the Russian Federation Concerning State Regulation of Merchant Shipping through the Water Area of the Northern Sea Route." Available at: http://asmp.morflot.ru/en/zakon_o_smp/

Fomina, Olesya 2013. Bol'shye problemy malykh narodov Severa obsuzhdayut na Yamale [Big problems of small nations are being discussed on Yamal], 29 March, http://www.vest i.ru/doc.html?id=1067747

Gavrilov, Yuri. 2014. 'Sever' Arktiki [The Arctic's 'North'], *Rossiyskaya Gazeta,* 1 December, http://www.rg.ru/2014/12/01/k omandovanie-site.html

Gizewski, P. 1995. Military Activity and Environmental Security: The Case of Radioactivity in the Arctic. In DeBardeleben, J. And J. Hannigan (eds.). Environmental Security and Quality after Communism: Eastern Europe and the Soviet Successor States. Boulder: Westview Press, pp. 25–41.

Gorenburg, Dmitry. 2011. Russia's Arctic Security Strategy. Russian Analytical Digest 96, 12 May, pp. 11–13.

Government of the Russian Federation. 2001. Osnovy Gosudarstvennoi Politiki Rossiiskoi Federatsii v Arktike [Foundations of the State Policy of the Russian Federation in the Arctic]. http://severnash.ru/economics/93-osnovy-gosudarstvennoy-politiki-rossiyskoy-federacii-v-arktike.html

The Government of the Russian Federation. 2014. Sotsial'no-Ekonomicheskoe Razvitie Arkticheskoy Zony Rossiyskoi Federatsii na Period do 2020 Goda [Socio-Economic Development of the Arctic Zone of the Russian Federation for the Period up to 2020]. http://government.ru/media/files/AtEYgOHutVc.pdf

Grigoriev, Y. (2010). Brussel' Gotovitsya k Bitveza Arktiku. Islandiu v Speshnom Poryadke Prinimayut v Evrosouyz [Brussels is Preparing Itself for the Fight for the Arctic. Iceland to Urgently Accede the EU]. Nezavisimaya gazeta, July 28. http://www.ng.ru/world/ 2010–07–28/1_arctic.html (in Russian).

Heininen, Lassi. 2001. "Ideas and Outcomes: Finding a Concrete Form for the Northern Dimension Initiative." The Northern Dimension: Fuel for the EU? Edited by Hanna Ojanen. Program on the Northern Dimension of the CFSP. Ulkopoliittineninstituutti&Institut fur Europaische Politik. Kauhava, pp. 20–53.

Heininen, Lassi. 2004. "Circumpolar International Relations and Geopolitics". Arctic Human Development Report. Akureyri: Stefansson Arctic Institute, pp. 207–225.

Heininen, Lassi. 2011. Arctic Strategies and Policies—Inventory and Comparative Study. The Northern Research Forum &The University of Lapland. Akureyri, Iceland August 2011.

Heininen, Lassi. 2012. "The End of the post-Cold War in the Arctic." Nordia Geographical Publications, Volume 40: 4. NGP Yearbook 2011 "Sustainable Development in the Arctic region though peace and stability". Geographical Society of Northern Finland. Tornio, 31–42.

Heininen, Lassi (2014). "Northern Geopolitics: Actors, Interests and Processes in the Circumpolar Arctic." Polar Geopolitics: Knowledges, Resources and Legal Regimes. Edited by Richard C. Powell and Klaus Dodds. Edward Elgar: Cheltenham, UK and Northampton, Massachusetts, pp. 241–258.

Heininen, Lassi (2013). "Arctic Security—Global Dimensions and Challenges, and National Policy Responses." The Yearbook of Polar Law 2013, Volume 5. Edited by Gudmundur Alfredsson, Timo Koivurova and Adam Stepien. Leiden-Boston: Brill/Martinus Nijhoff Publishers, pp. 93–115.

Heininen, Lassi. 2015. "Security of the Global Arctic in Transformation—Relevant Changes in Problem Definition." Future Security of the Global Arctic. Defence, Sovereignty and Climate. Edited by Lassi Heininen. Palgrave Pivot: UK.

Heininen, Lassi and Segerstahl, Boris. 2002. «International Negotiations Aiming at a Reduction of Nuclear Risks in the Barents Sea Region.» In: Containing the Atom. International Negotiations on Nuclear Security and Safety. Edited by Rudolf Avenhaus, Victor Kremenyuk and Gunnar Sjostedt. Lexington Books. International Institute for Applied Systems Analysis. New York, pp. 243–270.

Heininen L., Sergunin A., Yarovoy G. 2014. Russian Strategies in the Arctic: Avoiding a New Cold War. Moscow: International Discussion Club "Valdai".

Hobbs, Heidi. 1994. *City Hall Goes Abroad: The Foreign Policy of Local Politics*. Thousand Oaks: Sage.

Hocking, Brian. 1993. *Localizing Foreign Policy, Non-central Governments and Multilayered Diplomacy*. London: Palgrave Macmillan.

Huebert, Rob. 2010. The Newly Emerging Arctic Security Environment. Calgary: Canadian Defense & Foreign Affairs Institute (CDFA Paper, March). http://www.cdfai.org/PDF/The%20Newly%20Emerging%20Arctic%20Security%20Environment.pdf

Huebert, Rob, Exner-Pirot, Heather, Lajeunesse, Adam and Jay Gulledge. 2012. Climate Change & International Security: the Arctic as a Bellwether. Arlington, VA: Center for Climate and Energy Solutions. http://www.c2es.org/docUploads/arctic-security-report.pdf

Hübner, Danuta. 2012. "Regional Policy after 2013. Towards new European Territorial Cooperation," *Baltic Sea States Subregional Co-operation Newsletter*, December: 1–2. Available at: www.bsssc.com/upload/dokumenty/f_377.pdf, accessed January 19, 2014.

Humpert, Malte. 2013. The Future of Arctic Shipping: A New Silk Road for China? Washington, DC: The Arctic Institute.

(2008). Ilulissat Declaration, Arctic Ocean Conference, May 28. http://arcticcouncil.org/filearchive/Ilulissat-declaration.pdf

Indzhiev, Artur. 2010. Bitva za Arktiku. Budet li Sever Russkim? [The Arctic Battle: Will the North be Russian?]. Moscow: Yauza/Eksmo.

The International Bering Sea Forum. 2006. Issues. http://www.beringseaforum.org/issues.html

International Institute for Strategic Studies. 2012. Russia in the Arctic: economic interests override military aspirations. Strategic Comments (43) November 26. https://www.iiss.org/e n/publications/strategic%20comments/sections/2012-bb59/ru ssia-in-the-arctic--economic-interests-override-militaryaspirat ions-76ab

Joenniemi, P., Sergunin, A. 2003. *Russia and European Union's Northern Dimension: Clash or Encounter of Civilizations?* Nizhny Novgorod: Nizhny Novgorod Sate Linguistic University Press.

Joenniemi, P., Sergunin, A. 2011. 'When Two Aspire to Become One: City-Twinning in Northern Europe', *Journal of Borderlands Studies* 26 (2), pp. 231–242.

Joenniemi, P., Sergunin, A. 2012. *Laboratories of European Integration: City-Twinning in Northern Europe*. Tartu: Peipsi Center for Transboundary Cooperation.

Joenniemi, P., Sergunin, A. 2014. 'Paradiplomacy as a Capacity-Building Strategy: The Case of Russia's Northwestern Subnational Actors', Problems of Post-Communism 61 (6), pp. 18–33.

Kaczynski, Vlad. 2007. "US-Russian Bering Sea Marine Border Dispute: Conflict over Strategic Assets, Fisheries and Energy Resources," Russian Analytical Digest (20), pp. 2–5, http://www.css.ethz.ch/publications/DetailansichtPubDB_EN? rec_id=1284

Karlusov, Vyacheslav. 2012. The arctic vector of Chinese globalization. http://russiancouncil.ru/en/inner/?id_4=268#top

Keating, Michael. 1999. *Paradiplomacy in Action*. London: Frank Cass.

Khramchikhin A. (2011) Voyenno-politicheskaya situatsiya v Arktike i stsenarii vozmozhnykh konfliktov [Military-political situation in Arctic regions and the scenario of possible conflicts]. *Arktika i Sever* [The Arctic and the North], 2, 1–15 http://narfu.ru/upload/iblock/7f9/grjopufvqlvzveqamx.pdf. (in Russian).

Khramchikhin A (2013) Stanet li Arktika teatrom voennykh deistviy po poslednemu peredelu mira" [Will the Arctic become a military theater for the final re-division of the world?] *Arktika i Sever* (10): 52–60 (in Russian).

Klett, T.R. and Gautier D.L. 2009. Assessment of Undiscovered Petroleum Resources of the Barents Sea Shelf: U.S. Geological Survey Fact Sheet 2009–3037. http://pubs.usgs.gov/fs/2009/3037/pdf/FS09–3037.pdf

Kochemasov, Y.V., Morgunov, B.A. and V.I. Solomatin. 2009. Ekologo-ekonomicheskaya Otsenka Perspectivy Razvitiya Arktiki [Ecological-economic Assessment of Perspectives of the Arctic's Development]. http://www.perspektivy.info/rus/ekob/arktika_perspektivy_razvitija_2009–04–24.htm

Kontorovich, A.E., Epov, M.I., Burshtein, L.M., Kaminskii, V.D., Kurchikov, A.R., Malyshev, N.A., Prischepa, O.M., Safronov, A.F., Stupakova, A.V., Suprunenko, O.I., 2010. Geology and hydrocarbon resources of the continental shelf in Russian Arctic seas and the prospects of their development. Russian Geology and Geophysics 51 (1), pp. 3–11.

Konyshev V., Sergunin A. (2010). Arktika na perekryostke geopoliticheskikh interesov. [The Arctic at the Crossroads of Geopolitical Interests. Mirovaya Ekonomika i Mezhdunarodnye Otnosheniya. [World Economy and International Relations], 9, 43–53 (in Russian).

Konyshev, V., Sergunin, A. (2011a). Arktika v Mezdunarodnoi Politike: Sotrudnichestvoili Sopernichestvo? [The Arctic in International Politics: Cooperation or Competition?]. Moscow: The Russian Institute for Strategic Studies (in Russian).

Konyshev, V., Sergunin, A. (2011b). Mezhdunarodnye Organizatsiii Sotrudnichestvo v Arktike [International Organizations and Cooperation in the Arctic]. Vestnik Mezhdunarodnykh Organizatsiy [Messenger of International Organizations], (3), 27–35 (in Russian).

Konyshev, V., Sergunin, A. (2011c). Remilitarizatsiya Arktikii Bezopasnost Rossii [Re-militarization of the Arctic and Russia's security]. Natzional'naya Bezopasnost [National Security], (3–4), 55–67 (in Russian).

Konyshev V., Sergunin A. 2014. "Russian Military Strategies in the High North." Security and Sovereignty in the North Atlantic—Small States, Middle Powers and their Maritime Interests. Edited by Lassi Heininen. Palgrave Pivot, 80–99.

Konyshev V., Sergunin A. (2012). The Arctic at the Crossroads of Geopolitical Interests. Russian Politics and Law, 2, 34–54.

Koptelov, Vladimir. 2012. Strategy for Denmark in the development of the Arctic. http://russiancouncil.ru/en/inner/?id_4=349#top

Kraska, James. 2009. "International Security and International Law in the Northwest Passage", Vanderbilt Journal of Transnational Law 42, 1109–1132.

2008. Kross-Polyarny Express [Circumpolar Express]. http://zubow.ru/page/1/225_1.shtml

Lukin Y. (2010). Veliky peredel Arktiki. [The Great Partition of the Arctic]. NArFU, Archangelsk (in Russian).

Laruelle, Marlene. 2014. Russia's Arctic Strategies and the Future of the Far North. Armonk, N.Y.: M.E. Sharpe, Inc.

Lasserre, Frederic, Le Roy, Jerome and Richard Garon. 2012. "Is there an arms race in the Arctic?" Journal of Military and Strategic Studies 14 (3&4), 1–56. http://www.google.ru/url?sa=t&rct=j&q=&esrc=s&source=web&cd=1&ved=0CCoQFjAA&url=http%3A%2F%2Fwww.jmss.org%2Fjmss%2Findex.php%2Fjmss%2Farticle%2Fdownload%2F496%2F492&ei=knbCUavUHMSE4ASWuYGoAQ&usg=AFQjCNE3PjQQcbTEOECv1O3bbaK_aB_VHg&bvm=bv.48175248,d.bGE&cad=rjt

Lepik, Katri-Liis. 2009. "Euroregions as Mechanisms for Strengthening Cross-Border Cooperation in the Baltic Sea Region," *TRAMES: Journal of the Humanities and Social Sciences* 13: 265–284.

Leshukov, Igor. 2000. Northern Dimension: interests and perceptions. In Lejins, Atis, Nackmayr, Jorg-Dietrich (eds.) The Northern Dimension: an assessment and future development. Riga: Latvian Institute of International Affairs, pp. 38–49.

Leshukov, Igor. 2001. Can the Northern Dimension Break the Vicious Circle of the Russia-EU Relations In: Ojanen, Hanna (ed.). The Northern Dimension: Fuel for the EU? Programme on the Northern Dimension of the CFSP. Helsinki: The Finnish Institute of International Affairs & Institut fur Europaische Politik, pp. 118–41.

Macalister, Terry. 2010. "Climate Change Could Lead to Arctic Conflict, Warns Senior NATO Commander", The Guardian, October 11.

Medvedev, Dmytry. 2008. Osnovy Gosudarstvennoi Politiki Rossiiskoi Federatsii v Arktike na Period do 2020 Goda i Dal'neishuiu Perspektivu [Foundations of the State Policy of the Russian Federation in the Arctic up to and Beyond 2020]. http://www.rg.ru/2009/03/30/arktika-osnovy-dok.html

Ministry of Foreign Affairs (of Denmark). 2011. Denmark, Greenland and the Faroe Islands: Kingdom of Denmark Strategy for the Arctic 2011–2020. Copenhagen, August 2011.

Moe, Arild. 2014. Russia's Arctic continental shelf claim: A slow burning fuse? In Mark Nuttall and Anita DeyNuttall (eds.). Geopolitical and legal aspects of Canada's and Europe's Northern Dimensions. Edmonton: CCI Press.

Moe, Arild and Oystein Jensen. 2010. Opening of New Arctic Shipping Routes. Standard Briefing. Brussels: Directorate-General for External Policies of the Union/European Parliament.

Murashko, Olga. 2009. "Why did the important events in the indigenous peoples' life take place in the atmosphere of alienation?" http://www.raipon.info/en/component/content/article/8-news/35-why-didthe-important-events-in-the-indigenous-peoples-life-take-place-in-the-atmosphere-of-alienation.html

Nadkarni, Vidya and Norma Noonan, eds. 2013. *Emerging Powers in a Comparative Perspective: The Political and Economic Rise of the BRIC countries*. New York: Bloomsbury, 2013.

2013. National Strategy for the Arctic Region. Washington: Governmental Printing Office. http://www.whitehouse.gov/sites/d efault/files/docs/nat_arctic_strategy.pdf

Naumov, Valery and Inga Nikulkina. 2012. Osobennosty Razvitiya Rossiyskoi Arkitiki [Specifics of the Russian Arctic's Development]. http://sdo.rea.ru/cde/conference/3/file.php?fileId=54

Nenashev, Mikhail. 2010. "Arktichesky Region v Rossiyskoi Gosudarstvennosti" [The Arctic Region in Russia's Statehood]. Vlast' (10), 7–10.

Nilsen, Thomas. 2015. "Sanctions against Russia have cost Exxon Mobil $1 billion", Barents Observer, March 4, http://baren tsobserver.com/en/energy/2015/03/sanctions-have-cost-exx onmobil-1bn-03-03

Nordic Council of Ministers, *Guidelines for the Nordic Council of Ministers' Co-operation with North-West Russia 2009–2013* (2009), 2–3. Available at: www.norden.org/en/nordic-council-of-ministers/ministers-for-co-operation-mr-sam/russia/docume nts/guidelines-for-the-nordic-council-of-ministers-co-operation -with-northwest-russia, accessed September 12, 2012.

Nordic Environment Finance Corporation. 2013. Environmental Hot Spots in the Barents Region. http://www.nefco.org/e n/financing/environmental_hot_spots_in_ the_barents_region

North-Western Strategic Partnership. 2011. Strategiya Razvitiya Arkticheskoi Zony Rossiyskoi Federatsiii Obespecheniya Natsional'noi Bezopasnosti na Period do 2020 Goda. Proekt [The Strategy for the Development of the Arctic Zone of the Russian Federation and Ensuring National Security for the Period up to 2020.Draft]. St. Petersburg. http://www.n-west.ru/2011–01–20_1/

The Northern Sea Route Administration. 2013. Application for Admission to navigate through the Northern Sea Route Area. Available at: http://asmp.morflot.ru/files/fileslist/2013082113 3955en-20130716120054en-Application%20for%20Admissio n%20to%20navigate%20in%20the%20NSR.doc

Nye, Joseph. 2004. *Soft Power: The Means to Success in World Politics.* New York: Public Affairs.

2012. *Obshee Prostranstvo Sosedstva* [Neighborhood Common Space]. Available at: http://www.kolarcticenpi.info/c/documen t_library/get_file?folderId=101794&name=DLFE-8618.pdf, accessed March 25, 2014.

Odgaard, Liselotte. 2012. *China and Coexistence: Beijing's National Security Strategy for the 21st Century.* Washington, D.C: Woodrow Wilson Center Press/Johns Hopkins University Press, 2012.

Ol'shevski, Alexander. 2013. The speech of the Director of the Northern Sea Route Administration at the academic conference in the Institute of World Economy and International Relations, Russian Academy of Science, 30 September.

Olson, Carl L., Seidenberg, Mark J. and Selle, Robert W. (1998). "US-Russian maritime boundary giveaway", Orbis 42 (1), pp. 74–89.http://go.galegroup.com/ps/i.do?id=GALE%7CA2 0632370&v=2.1&u=stpe&it=r&p=ITOF&sw=w

Oreshenkov, Alexander. 2009. "Arctic Diplomacy," Russia in Global Affairs, (4) October-December. http://eng.globalaffai rs.ru/number/n_14250

- Oreshenkov, Alexander. 2010. "Arctic Square of Opportunities," Russia in Global Affairs, (4) October-December. http://eng.globalaffairs.ru/number/Arctic-Square-of-Opportun ities-15085

- Organski, A.F.K. 1958. *World Politics*. New York: Alfred and Knopf.

- Palamar', Nikolay. 2009. "Nekotorye Aspekty Pogranichnogo Razgranicheniia Mezhdu Rossiiskoi Federatsiei I SShA" [Some Aspects of Boundary Delimitation Between the Russian Federation and the USA]. Znanie. Ponimanie. Umenie (6). http://www.zpu-journal.ru/ezpu/2009/6/Palamar_Boundary_ Differentiation/index. php?sphrase_id=4718

Perkmann, Markus. 2003. "Cross-border Regions in Europe: Significance and Drivers of Regional Cross-border Cooperation," *European Urban and Regional Studies* 10 (2): 153–171

Plumer, B. (2012). Arctic sea ice just hit a record low. The Washington Post, August 28. URL: http://www.washingtonpost .com/blogs/wonkblog/wp/2012/08/28/arctic-sea-ice-just-hit-a-record-low-heres-why-itmatters/

(2013) President Putin makes tough statement on Arctic security to youth voters. *Chicago Tribune,* 3 December. Available at: http://www.chicagotribune.com/news/sns-rt-us-al-russia-putin-arctic-20131203,0,5499339.story (accessed 20 April 2014).

2010. Prirodnye Resursy Arktiki [The Arctic Natural Resources]. http://ria.ru/arctic_spravka/20100415/220120223.html

Putin, Vladimir. 2011. Vladimir Putin's speech at the second International Arctic Forum, September 23. http://arctic.ru/news/2011/09/vladimir-putins-speech-second-international-arctic-forum

Putin, Vladimir. 2012a. Ukaz Prezidenta RF ot 7 Maya 2012 No. 605 "O merakh po realizatsii vneshnepoliticheskogo kursa Rossiyskoi Federatsii" [Decree of the President of the RF, 7 May 2012, No. 605 "On the measures on the implementation of the Russian Federation's foreign policy course"] http://text.document.kremlin.ru/SESSION/PILOT/main.htm (in Russian).

Putin, Vladimir. 2012b. Vystuplenie na soveschanii poslov i postoyannykh predstavitelei Rossii, 9 Iulya 2012 [Speech at the meeting of Russian ambassadors and permanent representatives] http://www.kremlin.ru/news/15902 (in Russian).

Putin, Vladimir. 2013. Strategiya Razvitiya Arkticheskoi Zony Rossiyskoi Federatsiii Obespecheniya Natsional'noi Bezopasnosti na Period do 2020 Goda [The Strategy for the Development of the Arctic Zone of the Russian Federation and Ensuring National Security for the Period up to 2020]. Approved by President Vladimir Putin on February 20, 2013 http://правительство.рф/docs/22846/

Putin, Vladimir. 2014. O sukhoputnykh territoriyakh Arkticheskoy Zony Rossiyskoi Federatsii [On the land territories of the Arctic Zone of the Russian Federation]. The Decree of the President of the Russian Federation, 2 May 2014, http://graph.document.kremlin.ru/page.aspx?1;3631997

Ragner, Claes Lykke, ed. 2000. The 21st Century—Turning Point for the Northern Sea Route? Oslo: Kluwer Academic Publishers.

2009. Resolution of the 6th Congress of the indigenous peoples of the North, Siberia and Far East of the Russian Federation, Moscow, 24 April, http://raipon.info/en/the-vi-congress.html

Rogova, Anastasiya. 2008. *From Rejection to Re-embracement: Language and Identity of the Russian Speaking Minority in Kirkenes, Norway*. Kirkenes: Barents Institute.

Rogova, Anastasiya. 2009. "Chicken Is Not a Bird—Kirkenes Is Not Abroad: Borders and Territories in Perception of the Population in a Russian–Norwegian Borderland." *Journal of Northern Studies*, no. 1: 31–42.

Rosenstein, M. (ed.) 2009. Swords and Ploughshares Global Security, Climate Change, and the Arctic. Champaign: Program in Arms Control, Disarmament, and International Security, University of Illinois. URL: http://acdis.illinois.edu/assets/docs/505/GlobalSecurityClimateChangeandtheArctic.pd>

2013. The rules of navigation through the water area of the Northern Sea Route. Approved by the order of the Ministry of Transport of Russia, January 17, 2013, № 7.Available at: http://asmp.morflot.ru/files/fileslist/20130725190332en-Rules_Perevod_CNIIMF-25-04.pdf

(2009) Russia fears missile defense in the Arctic, September 29. Available at: http://www.upi.com/Top_News/2009/09/29/Russia-fears-missile-defenses-in-Arctic/UPI-80901254231286/#ixzz2TStTQULu80901254231286/#ixzz2TStTQULu (accessed 12 June 2015).

Ryabova, Larisa. 2010. "Community Viability and Well-Being in the Circumpolar North." In Globalization and the Circumpolar North, edited by Lassi Heininen and Chris Southcott, 119–147. Fairbanks: University of Alaska Press.

Savel'eva, Svetlana and Anton Savel'ev. 2010. "Spatial Reorientation of the National Interests of Russia." [Prostranstvennaya pereorientatsiya natsional'nyh interesov Rossii], Vestnik MGTU 13, no. 1, pp. 73–76.

Scheffer, Jaap de Hoop. 2009. Speech by NATO Secretary General on security prospects in the High North. January 29. http://www.nato.int/cps/en/SID-77003E4C-F5A7B982/natoliv e/opinions_50077.htm?selectedLocale=en

Schepp, Matthias and Gerald Traufetter. 2009. "Riches at the North Pole: Russia Unveils Aggressive Arctic Plans," Spiegel Online International, January 29. http://www.spiegel.de/i nternational/world/riches-atthe-north-pole-russia-unveils-aggr essive-arctic-plans-a-604338.html

Sergunin, Alexander. 2006. *Kaliningrad and the Euroregions.* Nizhny Novgorod: Nizhny Novgorod State Linguistic University Press.

Shaparov, Alexander. 2013. NATO i Novaya Povestka Dnya v Arktike [NATO and the New Arctic Agenda], http://russ iancouncil.ru/inner/?id_4=2375#top

(2013) Shoigu sozdast arkticheskuyu gruppirovku voisk [Shoigu will create an Arctic Group of Forces], 10 December. Available at: http://lenta.ru/news/2013/12/10/arctic/ (accessed 20 April 2014) (in Russian).

Smith, Mark and Keir Giles. 2007. Russia and the Arctic: "The last Dash North". Shrivenham: Defense Academy of the United Kingdom (Russia Series 07/26).

Soldatos, Panayotis. 1990. "An Explanatory Framework for the Study of Federal States as Foreign-policy Actors" in *Federalism and International Relations: the Role of Subnational Units*, ed. Hans Michelmann and Panayotis Soldatos. Oxford: Claredon Press, 34–53.

State Department Watch. 2009. 1990 U.S.-Soviet Executive Agreement on Maritime Boundary. http://statedepartment watch.org/1990ExecAgreement.htm

State Duma of the Russian Federation. 2002. Postanovlenie Gosudarstvennoy Dumy Federal'nogo Sobraniya Rossiyskoi Federatsiiot 14 Iyulya 2002 g. № 2880-III GD «O Posledstviyakh Primeneniya Soglasheniya Mezhdu Soyuzom Sovetskikh Sotsialisticheskikh Respublik i Soedinennymi Shtatami Ameriki o Linii Razgranicheniya Morskikh Prostranstv 1990 Goda dlya Natsional'nykh Interesov Rossiyskoi Federatsii" [Resolution of the State Duma of the Federal Assembly of the Russian Federation, July 14, 2002, № 2880-III GD "On the Implications of the Provisional Implementation of the Agreement Between the Union of Soviet Socialist Republics and the United States of America on the Line of Demarcation of Maritime Spaces of 1990 for National Interests of the Russian Federation"]. http://zakon.law7.ru/base68/part1/d68ru1536.htm

Stepanov, Igor, Orebech Peter and Douglas R. Brubaker. 2005. Legal Implications for the Russian Northern Sea Route and Westward in the Barents Sea. Oslo: The Fridtjof Nansen Institute. http://fni.no/doc&pdf/FNI-R0405.pdf

Tammen, Ronald L. et al. 2000. *Power Transitions: Strategies for the 21st Century*. New York: Seven Bridges Press.

Tkachenko, Stanislav. 2000. Rashirenie ES I voprosy bezopasnosti Rossii [EU enlargement and Russia's security concerns]. In Trenin, Dmitri (ed.). Rossiyai osnovnye instituty bezopasnosti v Evrope: vstupaya v XXI vek [Russia and the main European security institutions: approaching the 21st century]. Moscow: Moscow Carnegie Centre, 2000, pp. 49–75.

Trenin D., Bayev P. (2010). The Arctic: A View From Moscow. Moscow: Moscow Carnegie Centre.

(2010). Treaty between the Kingdom of Norway and the Russian Federation concerning Maritime Delimitation and Cooperation in the Barents Sea and the Arctic Ocean, Nor.-Russ., Sept. 15, 2010. http://www.regjeringen.no/upload/UD/Vedlegg/Folkerett/avtale_engelsk.pdf

(1920). Treaty Concerning the Archipelago of Spitsbergen [Svalbard Treaty], Feb. 9, 1920, 43 Stat. 1892, 2 L.N.T.S. 7. http://www.sysselmannen.no/The_Svalbard_Treaty_9ssFy.pdf.file

United Nations (1958). Convention on the Continental Shelf, Apr. 29, 1958, 499 U.N.T.S. 311. http://untreaty.un.org/ilc/texts/instruments/english/conventions/ 8_1_1958_continental_shelf.pdf

United Nations (1982).United Nations Convention on the Law of the Sea, Dec. 10, 1982, 1833 U.N.T.S. 397. http://www.un.org/Depts/los/convention_ agreements/texts/unclos/unclos_e.pdf

United Nations. 1987. 'Chapter 2: Towards Sustainable Development'. A/42/427. *Our Common Future: Report of the World Commission on Environment and Development.* New York: United Nations, http://www.un-documents.net/ocf-02.htm

(2014) *The United States Navy Arctic Roadmap for 2014 to 2030.* February 2014. Washington, DC: Chief of Naval Operations.

UPI. 2009. Russia fears missile defense in the Arctic. 29 September. http://www.upi.com/Top_News/2009/09/29/Russia-fears-missile-defenses-in-Arctic/UPI-80901254231286/#ixzz2TStTQULu80901254231286/#ixzz2TStTQULu

U.S. Department of Defense. 2013. Arctic Strategy. Washington, DC: Department of Defense. http://www.defense.gov/pubs/2013_Arctic_Strategy.pdf

U.S. Department of State. 2009. Status of Wrangel and Other Arctic Islands. September 8. http://www.state.gov/p/eur/rls/fs/128740.htm

U.S. Department of State. 2015. One Arctic: Shared Opportunities, Challenges and Responsibilities. U.S. Chairmanship of the Arctic Council, http://www.state.gov/e/oes/ocns/opa/arc/uschair/index.htm

U.S. Geological Survey. 2008. Circum-Arctic Resource Appraisal: Estimates of Undiscovered Oil and Gas North of the Arctic Circle. http://pubs.usgs.gov/fs/2008/3049/fs2008-3049.pdf

Voronkov, Lev. 2012. Interesy Rossii v Arktike [Russia's Interests in the Arctic].http://russiancouncil.ru/inner/?id_4=732#top

Vylegzhanin, Alexander. 2010. "20 Let 'Vremennogo Primeneniya' Soglasheniya Mezhdu SSSR i SShA o Linii Razgranichenia Morskikh Prostranstv" [20 Years of "Provisional Implementation" of the Agreement Between the USSR and the USA on the Line of Demarcation of Maritime Spaces], Vestnik MGIMO Universiteta (1), pp. 1–10. http://www.vestnik.mgimo.ru/fileserver/10/vestnik_10-11_vilegzhanin.pdf

Wellmann, Christian. 1998. "Introduction." In *From Town to Town. Local Actors as Transnational Actors,* Wellmann, Christian, ed. Hamburg: LIT Verlag: 9–14.

Wezeman, Siemon T. Military Capabilities in the Arctic. SIPRI Background Paper, March 2012.

Willett, Lee. 2009. The Navy in Russia's "Resurgence". RUSI Journal, 154: 1, pp. 50–55.

Wittkopf, Eugene R. 1997. *World Politics: Trend and Transformation.* New York: St. Martin's Press.

Yarovoy, Gleb. 2014. "Russia's Arctic Policy: Continuity and Changes." International Relations and the Arctic: Understanding Policy and Governance. Eds. by Robert Murray and Anita DeyNuttall. Cambria Press.

Zagorsky (ed.). 2011. Arktika: Zona Mira i Sotrudnichestva [The Arctic: Zone of Peace and Cooperation]. Moscow: Institute of World Economy and International Relations, Russian Academy of Sciences.

Zagorsky, Andrei. 2013. Arkticheskie ucheniya Severnogoplota [The Arctic exercises of the Northern Fleet]. http://www.imemo.ru/ru/publ/comments/2013/comm_2013_053.pdf (in Russian).

Zysk Katarzyna. 2008. Russian Military Power and the Arctic. Russian Foreign Policy (EU–Russia Centre's Review) 8, pp. 80–86.

SOVIET AND POST-SOVIET POLITICS AND SOCIETY

Edited by Dr. Andreas Umland

ISSN 1614-3515

1   Андреас Умланд (ред.)
    Воплощение Европейской
    конвенции по правам человека в
    России
    Философские, юридические и
    эмпирические исследования
    ISBN 3-89821-387-0

2   Christian Wipperfürth
    Russland – ein vertrauenswürdiger
    Partner?
    Grundlagen, Hintergründe und Praxis
    gegenwärtiger russischer Außenpolitik
    Mit einem Vorwort von Heinz Timmermann
    ISBN 3-89821-401-X

3   Manja Hussner
    Die Übernahme internationalen Rechts
    in die russische und deutsche
    Rechtsordnung
    Eine vergleichende Analyse zur
    Völkerrechtsfreundlichkeit der Verfassungen
    der Russländischen Föderation und der
    Bundesrepublik Deutschland
    Mit einem Vorwort von Rainer Arnold
    ISBN 3-89821-438-9

4   Matthew Tejada
    Bulgaria's Democratic Consolidation
    and the Kozloduy Nuclear Power Plant
    (KNPP)
    The Unattainability of Closure
    With a foreword by Richard J. Crampton
    ISBN 3-89821-439-7

5   Марк Григорьевич Меерович
    Квадратные метры, определяющие
    сознание
    Государственная жилищная политика в
    СССР. 1921 – 1941 гг
    ISBN 3-89821-474-5

6   Andrei P. Tsygankov, Pavel
    A.Tsygankov (Eds.)
    New Directions in Russian
    International Studies
    ISBN 3-89821-422-2

7   Марк Григорьевич Меерович
    Как власть народ к труду приучала
    Жилище в СССР – средство управления
    людьми. 1917 – 1941 гг.
    С предисловием Елены Осокиной
    ISBN 3-89821-495-8

8   David J. Galbreath
    Nation-Building and Minority Politics
    in Post-Socialist States
    Interests, Influence and Identities in Estonia
    and Latvia
    With a foreword by David J. Smith
    ISBN 3-89821-467-2

9   Алексей Юрьевич Безугольный
    Народы Кавказа в Вооруженных
    силах СССР в годы Великой
    Отечественной войны 1941-1945 гг.
    С предисловием Николая Бугая
    ISBN 3-89821-475-3

10 Вячеслав Лихачев и Владимир
    Прибыловский (ред.)
    Русское Национальное Единство,
    1990-2000. В 2-х томах
    ISBN 3-89821-523-7

11 Николай Бугай (ред.)
    Народы стран Балтии в условиях
    сталинизма (1940-е – 1950-е годы)
    Документированная история
    ISBN 3-89821-525-3

12 Ingmar Bredies (Hrsg.)
    Zur Anatomie der Orange Revolution
    in der Ukraine
    Wechsel des Elitenregimes oder Triumph des
    Parlamentarismus?
    ISBN 3-89821-524-5

13 Anastasia V. Mitrofanova
    The Politicization of Russian
    Orthodoxy
    Actors and Ideas
    With a foreword by William C. Gay
    ISBN 3-89821-481-8

14 Nathan D. Larson
    Alexander Solzhenitsyn and the
    Russo-Jewish Question
    ISBN 3-89821-483-4

15 Guido Houben
    Kulturpolitik und Ethnizität
    Staatliche Kunstförderung im Russland der
    neunziger Jahre
    Mit einem Vorwort von Gert Weisskirchen
    ISBN 3-89821-542-3

16 Leonid Luks
    Der russische „Sonderweg"?
    Aufsätze zur neuesten Geschichte Russlands
    im europäischen Kontext
    ISBN 3-89821-496-6

17 Евгений Мороз
    История «Мёртвой воды» – от
    страшной сказки к большой
    политике
    Политическое неоязычество в
    постсоветской России
    ISBN 3-89821-551-2

18 Александр Верховский и Галина
    Кожевникова (ред.)
    Этническая и религиозная
    интолерантность в российских СМИ
    Результаты мониторинга 2001-2004 гг.
    ISBN 3-89821-569-5

19 Christian Ganzer
    Sowjetisches Erbe und ukrainische
    Nation
    Das Museum der Geschichte des Zaporoger
    Kosakentums auf der Insel Chortycja
    Mit einem Vorwort von Frank Golczewski
    ISBN 3-89821-504-0

20 Эльза-Баир Гучинова
    Помнить нельзя забыть
    Антропология депортационной травмы
    калмыков
    С предисловием Кэролайн Хамфри
    ISBN 3-89821-506-7

21 Юлия Лидерман
    Мотивы «проверки» и «испытания»
    в постсоветской культуре
    Советское прошлое в российском
    кинематографе 1990-х годов
    С предисловием Евгения Марголита
    ISBN 3-89821-511-3

22 Tanya Lokshina, Ray Thomas, Mary
    Mayer (Eds.)
    The Imposition of a Fake Political
    Settlement in the Northern Caucasus
    The 2003 Chechen Presidential Election
    ISBN 3-89821-436-2

23 Timothy McCajor Hall, Rosie Read
    (Eds.)
    Changes in the Heart of Europe
    Recent Ethnographies of Czechs, Slovaks,
    Roma, and Sorbs
    With an afterword by Zdeněk Salzmann
    ISBN 3-89821-606-3

24 Christian Autengruber
    Die politischen Parteien in Bulgarien
    und Rumänien
    Eine vergleichende Analyse seit Beginn der
    90er Jahre
    Mit einem Vorwort von Dorothée de Nève
    ISBN 3-89821-476-1

25 Annette Freyberg-Inan with Radu
    Cristescu
    The Ghosts in Our Classrooms, or:
    John Dewey Meets Ceauşescu
    The Promise and the Failures of Civic
    Education in Romania
    ISBN 3-89821-416-8

26 John B. Dunlop
    The 2002 Dubrovka and 2004 Beslan
    Hostage Crises
    A Critique of Russian Counter-Terrorism
    With a foreword by Donald N. Jensen
    ISBN 3-89821-608-X

27 Peter Koller
    Das touristische Potenzial von
    Kam''janec'–Podil's'kyj
    Eine fremdenverkehrsgeographische
    Untersuchung der Zukunftsperspektiven und
    Maßnahmenplanung zur
    Destinationsentwicklung des „ukrainischen
    Rothenburg"
    Mit einem Vorwort von Kristiane Klemm
    ISBN 3-89821-640-3

28 Françoise Daucé, Elisabeth Sieca-
    Kozlowski (Eds.)
    Dedovshchina in the Post-Soviet
    Military
    Hazing of Russian Army Conscripts in a
    Comparative Perspective
    With a foreword by Dale Herspring
    ISBN 3-89821-616-0

29   Florian Strasser
     Zivilgesellschaftliche Einflüsse auf die
     Orange Revolution
     Die gewaltlose Massenbewegung und die
     ukrainische Wahlkrise 2004
     Mit einem Vorwort von Egbert Jahn
     ISBN 3-89821-648-9

30   Rebecca S. Katz
     The Georgian Regime Crisis of 2003-
     2004
     A Case Study in Post-Soviet Media
     Representation of Politics, Crime and
     Corruption
     ISBN 3-89821-413-3

31   Vladimir Kantor
     Willkür oder Freiheit
     Beiträge zur russischen Geschichtsphilosophie
     Ediert von Dagmar Herrmann sowie mit
     einem Vorwort versehen von Leonid Luks
     ISBN 3-89821-589-X

32   Laura A. Victoir
     The Russian Land Estate Today
     A Case Study of Cultural Politics in Post-
     Soviet Russia
     With a foreword by Priscilla Roosevelt
     ISBN 3-89821-426-5

33   Ivan Katchanovski
     Cleft Countries
     Regional Political Divisions and Cultures in
     Post-Soviet Ukraine and Moldova
     With a foreword by Francis Fukuyama
     ISBN 3-89821-558-X

34   Florian Mühlfried
     Postsowjetische Feiern
     Das Georgische Bankett im Wandel
     Mit einem Vorwort von Kevin Tuite
     ISBN 3-89821-601-2

35   Roger Griffin, Werner Loh, Andreas
     Umland (Eds.)
     Fascism Past and Present, West and
     East
     An International Debate on Concepts and
     Cases in the Comparative Study of the
     Extreme Right
     With an afterword by Walter Laqueur
     ISBN 3-89821-674-8

36   Sebastian Schlegel
     Der „Weiße Archipel"
     Sowjetische Atomstädte 1945-1991
     Mit einem Geleitwort von Thomas Bohn
     ISBN 3-89821-679-9

37   Vyacheslav Likhachev
     Political Anti-Semitism in Post-Soviet
     Russia
     Actors and Ideas in 1991-2003
     Edited and translated from Russian by Eugene
     Veklerov
     ISBN 3-89821-529-6

38   Josette Baer (Ed.)
     Preparing Liberty in Central Europe
     Political Texts from the Spring of Nations
     1848 to the Spring of Prague 1968
     With a foreword by Zdeněk V. David
     ISBN 3-89821-546-6

39   Михаил Лукьянов
     Российский консерватизм и
     реформа, 1907-1914
     С предисловием Марка Д. Стейнберга
     ISBN 3-89821-503-2

40   Nicola Melloni
     Market Without Economy
     The 1998 Russian Financial Crisis
     With a foreword by Eiji Furukawa
     ISBN 3-89821-407-9

41   Dmitrij Chmelnizki
     Die Architektur Stalins
     Bd. 1: Studien zu Ideologie und Stil
     Bd. 2: Bilddokumentation
     Mit einem Vorwort von Bruno Flierl
     ISBN 3-89821-515-6

42   Katja Yafimava
     Post-Soviet Russian-Belarussian
     Relationships
     The Role of Gas Transit Pipelines
     With a foreword by Jonathan P. Stern
     ISBN 3-89821-655-1

43   Boris Chavkin
     Verflechtungen der deutschen und
     russischen Zeitgeschichte
     Aufsätze und Archivfunde zu den
     Beziehungen Deutschlands und der
     Sowjetunion von 1917 bis 1991
     Ediert von Markus Edlinger sowie mit einem
     Vorwort versehen von Leonid Luks
     ISBN 3-89821-756-6

44 *Anastasija Grynenko in
Zusammenarbeit mit Claudia Dathe*
Die Terminologie des Gerichtswesens
der Ukraine und Deutschlands im
Vergleich
Eine übersetzungswissenschaftliche Analyse
juristischer Fachbegriffe im Deutschen,
Ukrainischen und Russischen
Mit einem Vorwort von Ulrich Hartmann
ISBN 3-89821-691-8

45 *Anton Burkov*
The Impact of the European
Convention on Human Rights on
Russian Law
Legislation and Application in 1996-2006
With a foreword by Françoise Hampson
ISBN 978-3-89821-639-5

46 *Stina Torjesen, Indra Overland (Eds.)*
International Election Observers in
Post-Soviet Azerbaijan
Geopolitical Pawns or Agents of Change?
ISBN 978-3-89821-743-9

47 *Taras Kuzio*
Ukraine – Crimea – Russia
Triangle of Conflict
ISBN 978-3-89821-761-3

48 *Claudia Šabić*
"Ich erinnere mich nicht, aber L'viv!"
Zur Funktion kultureller Faktoren für die
Institutionalisierung und Entwicklung einer
ukrainischen Region
Mit einem Vorwort von Melanie Tatur
ISBN 978-3-89821-752-1

49 *Marlies Bilz*
Tatarstan in der Transformation
Nationaler Diskurs und Politische Praxis
1988-1994
Mit einem Vorwort von Frank Golczewski
ISBN 978-3-89821-722-4

50 *Марлен Ларюэль (ред.)*
Современные интерпретации
русского национализма
ISBN 978-3-89821-795-8

51 *Sonja Schüler*
Die ethnische Dimension der Armut
Roma im postsozialistischen Rumänien
Mit einem Vorwort von Anton Sterbling
ISBN 978-3-89821-776-7

52 *Галина Кожевникова*
Радикальный национализм в России
и противодействие ему
Сборник докладов Центра «Сова» за 2004-
2007 гг.
С предисловием Александра Верховского
ISBN 978-3-89821-721-7

53 *Галина Кожевникова и Владимир
Прибыловский*
Российская власть в биографиях I
Высшие должностные лица РФ в 2004 г.
ISBN 978-3-89821-796-5

54 *Галина Кожевникова и Владимир
Прибыловский*
Российская власть в биографиях II
Члены Правительства РФ в 2004 г.
ISBN 978-3-89821-797-2

55 *Галина Кожевникова и Владимир
Прибыловский*
Российская власть в биографиях III
Руководители федеральных служб и
агентств РФ в 2004 г.
ISBN 978-3-89821-798-9

56 *Ileana Petroniu*
Privatisierung in
Transformationsökonomien
Determinanten der Restrukturierungs-
Bereitschaft am Beispiel Polens, Rumäniens
und der Ukraine
Mit einem Vorwort von Rainer W. Schäfer
ISBN 978-3-89821-790-3

57 *Christian Wipperfürth*
Russland und seine GUS-Nachbarn
Hintergründe, aktuelle Entwicklungen und
Konflikte in einer ressourcenreichen Region
ISBN 978-3-89821-801-6

58 *Togzhan Kassenova*
From Antagonism to Partnership
The Uneasy Path of the U.S.-Russian
Cooperative Threat Reduction
With a foreword by Christoph Bluth
ISBN 978-3-89821-707-1

59 *Alexander Höllwerth*
Das sakrale eurasische Imperium des
Aleksandr Dugin
Eine Diskursanalyse zum postsowjetischen
russischen Rechtsextremismus
Mit einem Vorwort von Dirk Uffelmann
ISBN 978-3-89821-813-9

60　Олег Рябов
«Россия-Матушка»
Национализм, гендер и война в России XX века
С предисловием Елены Гощило
ISBN 978-3-89821-487-2

61　Ivan Maistrenko
Borot'bism
A Chapter in the History of the Ukrainian Revolution
With a new introduction by Chris Ford
Translated by George S. N. Luckyj with the assistance of Ivan L. Rudnytsky
ISBN 978-3-89821-697-5

62　Maryna Romanets
Anamorphosic Texts and Reconfigured Visions
Improvised Traditions in Contemporary Ukrainian and Irish Literature
ISBN 978-3-89821-576-3

63　Paul D'Anieri and Taras Kuzio (Eds.)
Aspects of the Orange Revolution I
Democratization and Elections in Post-Communist Ukraine
ISBN 978-3-89821-698-2

64　Bohdan Harasymiw in collaboration with Oleh S. Ilnytzkyj (Eds.)
Aspects of the Orange Revolution II
Information and Manipulation Strategies in the 2004 Ukrainian Presidential Elections
ISBN 978-3-89821-699-9

65　Ingmar Bredies, Andreas Umland and Valentin Yakushik (Eds.)
Aspects of the Orange Revolution III
The Context and Dynamics of the 2004 Ukrainian Presidential Elections
ISBN 978-3-89821-803-0

66　Ingmar Bredies, Andreas Umland and Valentin Yakushik (Eds.)
Aspects of the Orange Revolution IV
Foreign Assistance and Civic Action in the 2004 Ukrainian Presidential Elections
ISBN 978-3-89821-808-5

67　Ingmar Bredies, Andreas Umland and Valentin Yakushik (Eds.)
Aspects of the Orange Revolution V
Institutional Observation Reports on the 2004 Ukrainian Presidential Elections
ISBN 978-3-89821-809-2

68　Taras Kuzio (Ed.)
Aspects of the Orange Revolution VI
Post-Communist Democratic Revolutions in Comparative Perspective
ISBN 978-3-89821-820-7

69　Tim Bohse
Autoritarismus statt Selbstverwaltung
Die Transformation der kommunalen Politik in der Stadt Kaliningrad 1990-2005
Mit einem Geleitwort von Stefan Troebst
ISBN 978-3-89821-782-8

70　David Rupp
Die Rußländische Föderation und die russischsprachige Minderheit in Lettland
Eine Fallstudie zur Anwaltspolitik Moskaus gegenüber den russophonen Minderheiten im „Nahen Ausland" von 1991 bis 2002
Mit einem Vorwort von Helmut Wagner
ISBN 978-3-89821-778-1

71　Taras Kuzio
Theoretical and Comparative Perspectives on Nationalism
New Directions in Cross-Cultural and Post-Communist Studies
With a foreword by Paul Robert Magocsi
ISBN 978-3-89821-815-3

72　Christine Teichmann
Die Hochschultransformation im heutigen Osteuropa
Kontinuität und Wandel bei der Entwicklung des postkommunistischen Universitätswesens
Mit einem Vorwort von Oskar Anweiler
ISBN 978-3-89821-842-9

73　Julia Kusznir
Der politische Einfluss von Wirtschaftseliten in russischen Regionen
Eine Analyse am Beispiel der Erdöl- und Erdgasindustrie, 1992-2005
Mit einem Vorwort von Wolfgang Eichwede
ISBN 978-3-89821-821-4

74　Alena Vysotskaya
Russland, Belarus und die EU-Osterweiterung
Zur Minderheitenfrage und zum Problem der Freizügigkeit des Personenverkehrs
Mit einem Vorwort von Katlijn Malfliet
ISBN 978-3-89821-822-1

75 Heiko Pleines (Hrsg.)
Corporate Governance in post-
sozialistischen Volkswirtschaften
ISBN 978-3-89821-766-8

76 Stefan Ihrig
Wer sind die Moldawier?
Rumänismus versus Moldowanismus in
Historiographie und Schulbüchern der
Republik Moldova, 1991-2006
Mit einem Vorwort von Holm Sundhaussen
ISBN 978-3-89821-466-7

77 Galina Kozhevnikova in collaboration
with Alexander Verkhovsky and
Eugene Veklerov
Ultra-Nationalism and Hate Crimes in
Contemporary Russia
The 2004-2006 Annual Reports of Moscow's
SOVA Center
With a foreword by Stephen D. Shenfield
ISBN 978-3-89821-868-9

78 Florian Küchler
The Role of the European Union in
Moldova's Transnistria Conflict
With a foreword by Christopher Hill
ISBN 978-3-89821-850-4

79 Bernd Rechel
The Long Way Back to Europe
Minority Protection in Bulgaria
With a foreword by Richard Crampton
ISBN 978-3-89821-863-4

80 Peter W. Rodgers
Nation, Region and History in Post-
Communist Transitions
Identity Politics in Ukraine, 1991-2006
With a foreword by Vera Tolz
ISBN 978-3-89821-903-7

81 Stephanie Solywoda
The Life and Work of
Semen L. Frank
A Study of Russian Religious Philosophy
With a foreword by Philip Walters
ISBN 978-3-89821-457-5

82 Vera Sokolova
Cultural Politics of Ethnicity
Discourses on Roma in Communist
Czechoslovakia
ISBN 978-3-89821-864-1

83 Natalya Shevchik Ketenci
Kazakhstani Enterprises in Transition
The Role of Historical Regional Development
in Kazakhstan's Post-Soviet Economic
Transformation
ISBN 978-3-89821-831-3

84 Martin Malek, Anna Schor-
Tschudnowskaja (Hrsg.)
Europa im Tschetschenienkrieg
Zwischen politischer Ohnmacht und
Gleichgültigkeit
Mit einem Vorwort von Lipchan Basajewa
ISBN 978-3-89821-676-0

85 Stefan Meister
Das postsowjetische Universitätswesen
zwischen nationalem und
internationalem Wandel
Die Entwicklung der regionalen Hochschule
in Russland als Gradmesser der
Systemtransformation
Mit einem Vorwort von Joan DeBardeleben
ISBN 978-3-89821-891-7

86 Konstantin Sheiko in collaboration
with Stephen Brown
Nationalist Imaginings of the
Russian Past
Anatolii Fomenko and the Rise of Alternative
History in Post-Communist Russia
With a foreword by Donald Ostrowski
ISBN 978-3-89821-915-0

87 Sabine Jenni
Wie stark ist das „Einige Russland"?
Zur Parteibindung der Eliten und zum
Wahlerfolg der Machtpartei
im Dezember 2007
Mit einem Vorwort von Klaus Armingeon
ISBN 978-3-89821-961-7

88 Thomas Borén
Meeting-Places of Transformation
Urban Identity, Spatial Representations and
Local Politics in Post-Soviet St Petersburg
ISBN 978-3-89821-739-2

89 Aygul Ashirova
Stalinismus und Stalin-Kult in
Zentralasien
Turkmenistan 1924-1953
Mit einem Vorwort von Leonid Luks
ISBN 978-3-89821-987-7

90 Leonid Luks
    Freiheit oder imperiale Größe?
    Essays zu einem russischen Dilemma
    ISBN 978-3-8382-0011-8

91 Christopher Gilley
    The 'Change of Signposts' in the
    Ukrainian Emigration
    A Contribution to the History of
    Sovietophilism in the 1920s
    With a foreword by Frank Golczewski
    ISBN 978-3-89821-965-5

92 Philipp Casula, Jeronim Perovic
    (Eds.)
    Identities and Politics
    During the Putin Presidency
    The Discursive Foundations of Russia's
    Stability
    With a foreword by Heiko Haumann
    ISBN 978-3-8382-0015-6

93 Marcel Viëtor
    Europa und die Frage
    nach seinen Grenzen im Osten
    Zur Konstruktion ‚europäischer Identität' in
    Geschichte und Gegenwart
    Mit einem Vorwort von Albrecht Lehmann
    ISBN 978-3-8382-0045-3

94 Ben Hellman, Andrei Rogachevskii
    Filming the Unfilmable
    Casper Wrede's 'One Day in the Life
    of Ivan Denisovich'
    Second, Revised and Expanded Edition
    ISBN 978-3-8382-0044-6

95 Eva Fuchslocher
    Vaterland, Sprache, Glaube
    Orthodoxie und Nationenbildung
    am Beispiel Georgiens
    Mit einem Vorwort von Christina von Braun
    ISBN 978-3-89821-884-9

96 Vladimir Kantor
    Das Westlertum und der Weg
    Russlands
    Zur Entwicklung der russischen Literatur und
    Philosophie
    Ediert von Dagmar Herrmann
    Mit einem Beitrag von Nikolaus Lobkowicz
    ISBN 978-3-8382-0102-3

97 Kamran Musayev
    Die postsowjetische Transformation
    im Baltikum und Südkaukasus
    Eine vergleichende Untersuchung der
    politischen Entwicklung Lettlands und
    Aserbaidschans 1985-2009
    Mit einem Vorwort von Leonid Luks
    Ediert von Sandro Henschel
    ISBN 978-3-8382-0103-0

98 Tatiana Zhurzhenko
    Borderlands into Bordered Lands
    Geopolitics of Identity in Post-Soviet Ukraine
    With a foreword by Dieter Segert
    ISBN 978-3-8382-0042-2

99 Кирилл Галушко, Лидия Смола
    (ред.)
    Пределы падения – варианты
    украинского будущего
    Аналитико-прогностические исследования
    ISBN 978-3-8382-0148-1

100 Michael Minkenberg (ed.)
    Historical Legacies and the Radical
    Right in Post-Cold War Central and
    Eastern Europe
    With an afterword by Sabrina P. Ramet
    ISBN 978-3-8382-0124-5

101 David-Emil Wickström
    Rocking St. Petersburg
    Transcultural Flows and Identity Politics in
    the St. Petersburg Popular Music Scene
    With a foreword by Yngvar B. Steinholt
    Second, Revised and Expanded Edition
    ISBN 978-3-8382-0100-9

102 Eva Zabka
    Eine neue „Zeit der Wirren"?
    Der spät- und postsowjetische Systemwandel
    1985-2000 im Spiegel russischer
    gesellschaftspolitischer Diskurse
    Mit einem Vorwort von Margareta Mommsen
    ISBN 978-3-8382-0161-0

103 Ulrike Ziemer
    Ethnic Belonging, Gender and
    Cultural Practices
    Youth Identitites in Contemporary Russia
    With a foreword by Anoop Nayak
    ISBN 978-3-8382-0152-8

104 Ksenia Chepikova
     ‚Einiges Russland' - eine zweite
     KPdSU?
     Aspekte der Identitätskonstruktion einer
     postsowjetischen „Partei der Macht"
     Mit einem Vorwort von Torsten Oppelland
     ISBN 978-3-8382-0311-9

105 Леонид Люкс
     Западничество или евразийство?
     Демократия или идеократия?
     Сборник статей об исторических дилеммах
     России
     С предисловием Владимира Кантора
     ISBN 978-3-8382-0211-2

106 Anna Dost
     Das russische Verfassungsrecht auf dem
     Weg zum Föderalismus und zurück
     Zum Konflikt von Rechtsnormen und
     -wirklichkeit in der Russländischen
     Föderation von 1991 bis 2009
     Mit einem Vorwort von Alexander Blankenagel
     ISBN 978-3-8382-0292-1

107 Philipp Herzog
     Sozialistische Völkerfreundschaft,
     nationaler Widerstand oder harmloser
     Zeitvertreib?
     Zur politischen Funktion der Volkskunst
     im sowjetischen Estland
     Mit einem Vorwort von Andreas Kappeler
     ISBN 978-3-8382-0216-7

108 Marlène Laruelle (ed.)
     Russian Nationalism, Foreign Policy,
     and Identity Debates in Putin's Russia
     New Ideological Patterns after the Orange
     Revolution
     ISBN 978-3-8382-0325-6

109 Michail Logvinov
     Russlands Kampf gegen den
     internationalen Terrorismus
     Eine kritische Bestandsaufnahme des
     Bekämpfungsansatzes
     Mit einem Geleitwort von
     Hans-Henning Schröder
     und einem Vorwort von Eckhard Jesse
     ISBN 978-3-8382-0329-4

110 John B. Dunlop
     The Moscow Bombings
     of September 1999
     Examinations of Russian Terrorist Attacks
     at the Onset of Vladimir Putin's Rule
     Second, Revised and Expanded Edition
     ISBN 978-3-8382-0388-1

111 Андрей А. Ковалёв
     Свидетельство из-за кулис
     российской политики I
     Можно ли делать добро из зла?
     (Воспоминания и размышления о
     последних советских и первых
     послесоветских годах)
     With a foreword by Peter Reddaway
     ISBN 978-3-8382-0302-7

112 Андрей А. Ковалёв
     Свидетельство из-за кулис
     российской политики II
     Угроза для себя и окружающих
     (Наблюдения и предостережения
     относительно происходящего после 2000 г.)
     ISBN 978-3-8382-0303-4

113 Bernd Kappenberg
     Zeichen setzen für Europa
     Der Gebrauch europäischer lateinischer
     Sonderzeichen in der deutschen Öffentlichkeit
     Mit einem Vorwort von Peter Schlobinski
     ISBN 978-3-89821-749-1

114 Ivo Mijnssen
     The Quest for an Ideal Youth in
     Putin's Russia I
     Back to Our Future! History, Modernity, and
     Patriotism according to Nashi, 2005-2013
     With a foreword by Jeronim Perović
     Second, Revised and Expanded Edition
     ISBN 978-3-8382-0368-3

115 Jussi Lassila
     The Quest for an Ideal Youth in
     Putin's Russia II
     The Search for Distinctive Conformism in the
     Political Communication of Nashi, 2005-2009
     With a foreword by Kirill Postoutenko
     Second, Revised and Expanded Edition
     ISBN 978-3-8382-0415-4

116 Valerio Trabandt
     Neue Nachbarn, gute Nachbarschaft?
     Die EU als internationaler Akteur am Beispiel
     ihrer Demokratieförderung in Belarus und der
     Ukraine 2004-2009
     Mit einem Vorwort von Jutta Joachim
     ISBN 978-3-8382-0437-6

117   Fabian Pfeiffer
       Estlands Außen- und Sicherheitspolitik I
       Der estnische Atlantizismus nach der
       wiedererlangten Unabhängigkeit 1991-2004
       Mit einem Vorwort von Helmut Hubel
       ISBN 978-3-8382-0127-6

118   Jana Podßuweit
       Estlands Außen- und Sicherheitspolitik II
       Handlungsoptionen eines Kleinstaates im
       Rahmen seiner EU-Mitgliedschaft (2004-2008)
       Mit einem Vorwort von Helmut Hubel
       ISBN 978-3-8382-0440-6

119   Karin Pointner
       Estlands Außen- und Sicherheitspolitik III
       Eine gedächtnispolitische Analyse estnischer
       Entwicklungskooperation 2006-2010
       Mit einem Vorwort von Karin Liebhart
       ISBN 978-3-8382-0435-2

120   Ruslana Vovk
       Die Offenheit der ukrainischen
       Verfassung für das Völkerrecht und
       die europäische Integration
       Mit einem Vorwort von Alexander
       Blankenagel
       ISBN 978-3-8382-0481-9

121   Mykhaylo Banakh
       Die Relevanz der Zivilgesellschaft
       bei den postkommunistischen
       Transformationsprozessen in mittel-
       und osteuropäischen Ländern
       Das Beispiel der spät- und postsowjetischen
       Ukraine 1986-2009
       Mit einem Vorwort von Gerhard Simon
       ISBN 978-3-8382-0499-4

122   Michael Moser
       Language Policy and the Discourse on
       Languages in Ukraine under President
       Viktor Yanukovych (25 February
       2010–28 October 2012)
       ISBN 978-3-8382-0497-0 (Paperback edition)
       ISBN 978-3-8382-0507-6 (Hardcover edition)

123   Nicole Krome
       Russischer Netzwerkkapitalismus
       Restrukturierungsprozesse in der
       Russischen Föderation am Beispiel des
       Luftfahrtunternehmens "Aviastar"
       Mit einem Vorwort von Petra Stykow
       ISBN 978-3-8382-0534-2

124   David R. Marples
       'Our Glorious Past'
       Lukashenka's Belarus and
       the Great Patriotic War
       ISBN 978-3-8382-0574-8 (Paperback edition)
       ISBN 978-3-8382-0675-2 (Hardcover edition)

125   Ulf Walther
       Russlands "neuer Adel"
       Die Macht des Geheimdienstes von
       Gorbatschow bis Putin
       Mit einem Vorwort von Hans-Georg Wieck
       ISBN 978-3-8382-0584-7

126   Simon Geissbühler (Hrsg.)
       Kiew – Revolution 3.0
       Der Euromaidan 2013/14 und die
       Zukunftsperspektiven der Ukraine
       ISBN 978-3-8382-0581-6 (Paperback edition)
       ISBN 978-3-8382-0681-3 (Hardcover edition)

127   Andrey Makarychev
       Russia and the EU
       in a Multipolar World
       Discourses, Identities, Norms
       With a foreword by Klaus Segbers
       ISBN 978-3-8382-0629-5

128   Roland Scharff
       Kasachstan als postsowjetischer
       Wohlfahrtsstaat
       Die Transformation des sozialen
       Schutzsystems
       Mit einem Vorwort von Joachim Ahrens
       ISBN 978-3-8382-0622-6

129   Katja Grupp
       Bild Lücke Deutschland
       Kaliningrader Studierende sprechen über
       Deutschland
       Mit einem Vorwort von Martin Schulz
       ISBN 978-3-8382-0552-6

130   Konstantin Sheiko, Stephen Brown
       History as Therapy
       Alternative History and Nationalist
       Imaginings in Russia, 1991-2014
       ISBN 978-3-8382-0665-3

131 Elisa Kriza
Alexander Solzhenitsyn: Cold War Icon, Gulag Author, Russian Nationalist?
A Study of the Western Reception of his Literary Writings, Historical Interpretations, and Political Ideas
With a foreword by Andrei Rogatchevski
ISBN 978-3-8382-0589-2 (Paperback edition)
ISBN 978-3-8382-0690-5 (Hardcover edition)

132 Serghei Golunov
The Elephant in the Room
Corruption and Cheating in Russian Universities
ISBN 978-3-8382-0570-0

133 Manja Hussner, Rainer Arnold (Hgg.)
Verfassungsgerichtsbarkeit in Zentralasien I
Sammlung von Verfassungstexten
ISBN 978-3-8382-0595-3

134 Nikolay Mitrokhin
Die "Russische Partei"
Die Bewegung der russischen Nationalisten in der UdSSR 1953-1985
Aus dem Russischen übertragen von einem Übersetzerteam unter der Leitung von Larisa Schippel
ISBN 978-3-8382-0024-8

135 Manja Hussner, Rainer Arnold (Hgg.)
Verfassungsgerichtsbarkeit in Zentralasien II
Sammlung von Verfassungstexten
ISBN 978-3-8382-0597-7

136 Manfred Zeller
Das sowjetische Fieber
Fußballfans im poststalinistischen Vielvölkerreich
Mit einem Vorwort von Nikolaus Katzer
ISBN 978-3-8382-0757-5

137 Kristin Schreiter
Stellung und Entwicklungspotential zivilgesellschaftlicher Gruppen in Russland
Menschenrechtsorganisationen im Vergleich
ISBN 978-3-8382-0673-8

138 David R. Marples, Frederick V. Mills (eds.)
Ukraine's Euromaidan
Analyses of a Civil Revolution
ISBN 978-3-8382-0660-8

139 Bernd Kappenberg
Setting Signs for Europe
Why Diacritics Matter for European Integration
With a foreword by Peter Schlobinski
ISBN 978-3-8382-0663-9

140 René Lenz
Internationalisierung, Kooperation und Transfer
Externe bildungspolitische Akteure in der Russischen Föderation
Mit einem Vorwort von Frank Ettrich
ISBN 978-3-8382-0751-3

141 Juri Plusnin, Yana Zausaeva, Natalia Zhidkevich, Artemy Pozanenko
Wandering Workers
Mores, Behavior, Way of Life, and Political Status of Domestic Russian Labor Migrants
Translated by Julia Kazantseva
ISBN 978-3-8382-0653-0

142 Matthew Kott, David J. Smith (eds.)
Latvia – A Work in Progress?
100 Years of State- and Nation-building
ISBN 978-3-8382-0648-6

143 Инна Чувычкина (ред.)
Экспортные нефте- и газопроводы на постсоветском пространстве
Анализ трубопроводной политики в свете теории международных отношений
ISBN 978-3-8382-0822-0

144 Johann Zajaczkowski
Russland – eine pragmatische Großmacht?
Eine rollentheoretische Untersuchung russischer Außenpolitik am Beispiel der Zusammenarbeit mit den USA nach 9/11 und des Georgienkrieges von 2008
Mit einem Vorwort von Siegfried Schieder
ISBN 978-3-8382-0837-4

145 Boris Popivanov
Changing Images of the Left in Bulgaria
The Challenge of Post-Communism in the Early 21st Century
ISBN 978-3-8382-0667-7

146 *Lenka Krátká*
A History of the Czechoslovak Ocean
Shipping Company 1948-1989
How a Small, Landlocked Country Ran
Maritime Business During the Cold War
ISBN 978-3-8382-0666-0

147 *Alexander Sergunin*
Explaining Russian Foreign Policy
Behavior
Theory and Practice
ISBN 978-3-8382-0752-0

148 *Darya Malyutina*
Migrant Friendships in
a Super-Diverse City
Russian-Speakers and their Social
Relationships in London in the 21st Century
With a foreword by Claire Dwyer
ISBN 978-3-8382-0652-3

149 *Alexander Sergunin, Valery Konyshev*
Russia in the Arctic
Hard or Soft Power?
ISBN 978-3-8382-0753-7

150 *John J. Maresca*
Helsinki Revisited
A Key U.S. Negotiator's Memoirs
on the Development of the CSCE into the
OSCE
With a foreword by Hafiz Pashayev
ISBN 978-3-8382-0852-7

ibidem-Verlag

Melchiorstr. 15

D-70439 Stuttgart

info@ibidem-verlag.de

www.ibidem-verlag.de
www.ibidem.eu
www.edition-noema.de
www.autorenbetreuung.de

Zeitfracht Medien GmbH
Ferdinand-Jühlke-Straße 7,
99095 - DE, Erfurt
produktsicherheit@zeitfracht.de